Finding Your Career Mojo

Kevin Kokinda

ISBN: 9798538389162

DEDICATION

You are only as good as the ones you surround yourself with and I have been fortunate to have them with me.

First, my wife and soul partner, Stacey who fell into my life and has opened up my eyes in so many ways.

My son Zach, who serves as a reminder to me of what is important in this world.
My daughter and angel, Michaela, who never got the chance to be her own voice, but still inspires me from the other side.

My immediate and extended family and friends who I can lean on in times of self-doubt.

The hundreds of HR and talent acquisition professionals whose valuable input (good, bad, or indifferent) has given me the confidence and conviction to share with job seekers.

Finally, all my clients! I hope that I was able to make some kind of difference. Many thanks for inspiring me to act like a shepherd… instead of a sheep.

CONTENTS

PREFACE

Driving to work on a bone-chilling morning in January, a new role was potentially awaiting me.

You see, for some time now, I thought I was being groomed for a management position. Hell, I shattered sales records, strived to lead by example, proactively took on managerial tasks, and even wrote a five-page 'manifesto' to illustrate how I was going to grow revenue within 90 days.

Ah yes….an impressive record indeed!

As I grabbed my morning cup of coffee my sales director called me into the office.

He seemed jovial as he invited me to sit down and after a few minutes of engaging in small talk, he went right to it.

"Kevin, you deserve complete transparency…We offered the position to someone else."

He explained that it wasn't because of my performance and I was one of two final candidates, further elaborating:

"We had an opportunity to snatch up this 'rock star' and it was simply too good for us to pass up."

Yes, these words cut thru me like a rusted razor, although they didn't surprise me either.

This wasn't the first time, I felt disappointment and rejection and it probably wasn't going to be the last time if I stayed on my current course.

Although it felt like my professional foundation had burnt to the ground…

From the ashes rose….

Resumedics!

And it was time to get MY career mojo back!

Finding Your Career Mojo

Chapter 1

Cheers To The Dreamers

Many of us have heard this term: Doing the same thing over and over hoping you're going to get a better result.

They call this… 'the definition of insanity!'

When it comes to resumés, it's been a long-standing perception to send out as many as possible or throw it up on a job site and wait for all those hiring managers to connect with us (Spray and Pray).

We are told to use powerful action verbs or any 'hook' to grab the attention of the hiring decision-maker.

Sound familiar?

Then, comes the initial interview screening.

Some job seekers will be diligent and invest some time researching the company and the position itself. (Best practice).

Others…will simply try and 'wing it.'

Or, as I call it, the art of bullshitting!

Interestingly, in a recent story by CNBC,* they have uncovered that some who have mastered the art of bullshitting show a high degree of intelligence.

However, even if these so-called bullshitters (or wingers) keep this process going until something breaks through…. is the job something they covet… or are they just settling?

Then, we have the dreamers…

Naturally, someone in my profession is frequently being asked two questions:
-   "How to structure my resumé to land that 'dream job'?"
-    "How can I land my dream job without any relevant experience?"

So, here is how I begin to formulate these answers:
-   For starters, I begin reviewing these 'dream job' postings.
-   From there, I am analyzing how their qualifications and tools align with these roles.

Many times, I am successful at extracting relevant skills from my clients they didn't even know they had!

Other times… I am not.

Then, with complete transparency…I give them my feedback.

Pretty straightforward, right?

When it comes to a job posting, I always like to think of it as an open-book quiz. The employer is giving you the answers…but you still need to locate them in the chapters.

Recently, I had an executive-level client who was struggling with getting responses from his resumé.

He was seeking higher-level roles in finance (controller, CFO, etc.) and was baffled that he was not being considered given his finance background and the companies he worked for.

When I asked him what his strategy was, he said he was posting his resumé to executive-level job boards, Indeed, Ladders, and LinkedIn, and reaching out to contacts he knows from certain work circles in addition to networking.

Well, the first items I am going to inquire about are the job postings he had applied to…and those he was considering applying for.

After reviewing his resumé and about six of the job postings, it was easy to find the disconnect.

Originally, his resumé was leading off with a summary that read like a biography and was very generalized. Some of his statements were structured like this:

- I have led finance teams and accountants to grow business.
- I communicate professionally with customers and management.
- I perform multiple tasks with creative thinking and improve business processes and tools.
- Seeking a finance leadership role demonstrating my skills and 20 years of demonstrated experience.

His work history did not exactly paint a picture of success either:

- Manage and give financial reports to the executive committee and partners each month.
- Execute and streamline policies, technology, procedures, controls, and most methodologies.
- Manage daily cash and prepare cash-flow reports, projecting cash needs each month.

After gathering some additional information, we both felt confident with his new summary that included the following items:

- That he was a hands-on finance director with over 20 years of progressive global leadership experience directing corporate management for multibillion-dollar enterprises.
- He specializes in capital markets, financial planning and analysis (FP&A), taxation, treasury, sales, technology implementation, and enterprise resource planning (ERP).
- Overseeing full profit and loss (P&L), and favorably positioning EBITDA.
- Promoting his ability to identify and analyze proposed transactions, and formulate business plans and actionable insights to advance a company's goals and mission in private equity and multinational environments.

More importantly, I extracted some notable cost-saving accomplishments, finance technology projects he led and highlighted these throughout his work history that includes the following:

- Successfully overhauled the company's tax strategy by utilizing alternative credits and previously unused tax-saving opportunities that led to the recovery of over $1.5 million in income tax overpayments.
- Introduced Salesforce Lightning CRM and SAP ERP software to generate advanced KPI metrics, provide accurate revenue forecasting, and more quantifiable dashboards to enhance multinational sales teams. These implementations have been a key driver in growing business by over $12 million.

This is what I call: Putting a resumé on steroids!

Another driver I look for is the value-added competencies that job seekers can use to their advantage.

Victor is a mid-level customer service specialist who is looking to rise to a leadership position. He meets most of the criteria for several job postings, but one glaring omittance from these roles is that they are not asking for any fluency in another language.

Well, guess what?

Victor, 'Habla Espanol' (Speaks Spanish)!

So, he would be remiss if he didn't put that on his resumé.

Value-added baby!

Sometimes, that dream job could be within the company. But the issue with that is many employees feel that their service time merits a shot at snagging that role.

And that is exactly what that is…a shot.

Sure, companies will interview them if they put in for it, but many times is it simply a courtesy.

Do you think they view that individual as a viable candidate?
Yes and no.

In my case, I put in the work and did everything that was
required…and still got the shaft.
Were they just jerking me around?
Perhaps.

Some, consistently earn excellent performance evaluations
but still get passed over (which I think sucks).
Typically, it is easy to blame it on favoritism, age, race, or
gender.
And sometimes, that is the case, unfortunately.

As I was putting together information for this book, there
has been an alarming number of job postings in all industries.
Many individuals simply elected not to go back to work,
because of new COVID variants, low wages, and the overhead
that comes with communicating to work.
Also, many employees have had a taste of working from
home, and they like it…they like it a lot!

Regardless of your situation, this may be an opportune time
to seek those dream roles!
But does that role only consist of working remotely from
home?
Also, do you feel that loyalty and hard work is the
framework for landing that dream job?
Unless someone has been isolated from the universe, or in
a deep coma, it's not breaking news that COVID has changed
the landscape of how employers and employees view
opportunities in the job market.

Some can look at it as free agency and take the approach that their background and skills are going to be more appreciated and lucrative with another company, with nothing holding them back.

Recruiters and talent acquisition managers are always aggressively seeking out these potential 'free agents' like a pack of wolves and have no shame in plucking a qualified individual right out from under the nose of another employer.

So, if you fall in the dreamer category, ask yourself…
"How dream job-ready am I?"

Jeanna has worked as a receptionist for a regional meat-packing facility for six years and has been taking courses to finish up her Bachelors' degree in Accounting, eventually working towards her CPA.

She has always considered herself a numbers geek and envisions working for a Big Four or corporate accounting firm crunching numbers, looking for tax loopholes, and presenting cost-saving strategies to executive-level stakeholders.

Although she is not a CPA yet, she can at least use her accounting degree to pivot into more advanced bookkeeping, AP/AR, finance management, and auditing roles.

More importantly, she now has the extra tools to apply for new accounting roles with a corporate company… or elect to negotiate an increase in salary and higher position with her current employer.

And if the competition for acquiring highly talented employees is fierce, Jeanna's employer should weigh that option considerably.

Otherwise, her services will be appreciated elsewhere!

Job markets, like stocks, are volatile and ambiguous.

However, if history has taught us anything it's that a robust employment market can be fleeting for job seekers.

Over time, certain opportunities become scarcer, windows close, and the competition for these 'dream jobs' becomes fiercer.

So, if you are trying to capture a unicorn…

Make sure you have your golden lasso at the ready!

Chapter 2

Fluffing, Stuffing, & Partaking

There is a confession I must make.

For a long time, I took soft skills for granted.

In fact, I use to advocate leaving most of them off a resumé.

I always referred to it as…

'Fluffing and Stuffing.'

Typically, it is common for job seekers to add 'fluff' at the top of the resumé, and if I had a dollar every time someone told me their strengths were working with people, solving problems, and multitasking…

I could live off the interest!

Furthermore, many hiring managers have told me they will shitcan a resumé in a New York minute if they see too much fluff.

There is also a fine line between illustrating these soft skills on paper, demonstrating them during an interview using a STAR methodology (recounting a situation, action, task, and result), or on a personality evaluation.

Many job seekers will have all kinds of soft skills listed on their resumé… yet have no idea how to parlay them into a new role.

I call this the 'safety net.'

This is a secure, all-encompassing method of keyword optimization covering familiar items, but hardly ever mastered by a job candidate.

And that is the fault of the employer!

They will litter every job posting with this fluff:
- Self-Motivation and Working Independently
- Working with multi-disciplinary or cross-functional teams
- Internal and External Relationships
- Oral and Written Communications
- Energetic, Dynamic, and Enthusiastic
- Time Management, Critical Thinking, and Decision' Making

Fortunately, there are effective ways to convey these soft skills on a resumé that will lend more credibility.

And it starts with the summary.

For example, if someone is seeking an office support role they could frame their soft skills like this:
- Highly adaptable and multi-faceted customer service specialist with over 10 years of cumulative experience in office administration, sales, and hospitality.

- Displays tremendous versatility to thrive in new roles in a fast-paced work environment. Self-motivated, who can lead by example with a demonstrated commitment to ongoing professional growth and development.

- Utilizes sound judgment, critical decision-making, and qualitative problem-solving to handle multiple tasks in a time-sensitive setting.

- Employs clear and influential communication techniques (written & verbal) to collaborate with cross-functional teams, manage and mentor staff members, and negotiate with vendors.

By weaving in the soft skills with the additional qualifications, they are at least attempting to portray these skills in a manner that may pique the interest of a hiring decision-maker instead of listing them separately to simply get past an applicant tracking system. (More on this as well).

Now I would like to take this time to elaborate on certain skills...

Like multitasking for instance.

One of the biggest misconceptions in today's workforce! I mean, what is a true multitasker anyway?

Typically, I like to illustrate this on a resumé as one who can perform and complete multiple tasks successfully in a deadline-driven environment.

When it comes to daily functions, for many of us it is common to be outstanding in one area...but very difficult to do this simultaneously with other tasks.

And you know what, that's okay!

If you can come close to handling multiple tasks simultaneously in a satisfactory manner, you are shooting par for the course!

In an interesting study conducted by David Strayer, a professor of psychology at the University of Utah, he concluded that only TWO PERCENT of us can juggle multiple tasks without sacrificing the quality of our work!*

Now, let's examine some newer soft skills that may be the most underappreciated and underutilized in the workplace today...

Positive culture, diversity, and inclusion.

Twenty years ago, did we even know what a positive workplace culture was? Or did we just think about it in another light?

If you are a Baby Boomer or Gen Xer, remember when smoking in the office and making inappropriate comments to a co-worker were not grounds for a major lawsuit?

Unfortunately, back then, there was little that an employee could do without creating waves.

Also, how much effort was made when it came to embracing race, gender, equality, diversity, or inclusion into the workforce?

I didn't recall HR rolling out any programs on it back in 1999.

In today's workforce, job candidates must demonstrate that they can implement AND embrace these skills in the workplace.

Especially if they are striving to serve in a leadership capacity.

In 2020 the Supreme Court ruled favorably in Bostock vs. Clayton County, concluding that LGBTQ individuals were protected from discrimination under Title VII of the Civil Rights Act of 1964.*

Although this landmark ruling was significant because they set more definitive parameters regarding color and LGBTQ discrimination, many still struggle with how to work within these frameworks in the workforce.

Whether it's religion, stupidity, media influence, or plain ignorance, it will be impossible to alter everyone's belief regarding another employees' sexual preference or the color of their skin, no matter how much effort HR puts into these programs.

In a cohesive work environment, what needs to be embraced is the example an employee is setting.

Regardless of a person's make-up, the main driver should be productivity, collaboration, and utilizing best practices.

And that warrants respect, regardless of classification!

It should be simple… right?

It's just too bad some try to make it so damn complex.

Something else to consider is that many who choose to discriminate could also be lacking career mojo.

They just don't realize it.

One of my favorite soft skills that can demonstrate the talents of a leader is emotional intelligence (EI).

Arguably the most challenging competency to master and a driving force in empowering and motivating individuals to perform at a higher level.

By utilizing this empathetic approach when engaging with others, an effective leader can guide their cognitive thinking and behavior pattern adjusting their emotions to adapt to different work environments and diverse individuals.

According to Wikipedia, this term was first coined in 1964.* However, its popularity stems from the 1995 best-selling book

'Emotional Intelligence,' written by science journalist Daniel Goleman,* who defines these characteristics as critical in driving leadership performance.*

When I counsel my executive-level clients, I frequently ask them 'why' instead of 'how' they advanced up the corporate ladder faster than their counterparts.

Almost all their answers had nothing to do with personal performance, timing, or revenue generation.

It was how they managed people.

Although some psychologists will contradict that EI is not a standard of intelligence, you will see Emotional IQ mentioned as a key requirement on many job postings.

These days many companies regard this as a vital component that is critical in determining leadership qualities and business success.

Elevating individuals to the next level in their careers is a core element in my line of service.

However, when they vent to me about struggling to achieve this, I typically notice several items related to EI absent on their resumé:

- How they motivate and empower individuals to perform at a higher level.
- Getting employees promoted internally.
- The ability to recruit and retain a quality workforce.

Think about how much a high employee turnover rate impacts a business's bottom line?

Worse, contributing to an organization with a track record for firing employees due to performance?

According to the Center for American Progress,* it is estimated that it costs an employer approximately 20% of that employee's salary to replace them once they leave (attrition or termination).

A couple of items that factor into this include:
- The hard costs associated with hiring a new person (advertising, interviewing, screening, & onboarding).
- The time it takes for a new hire to reach a predecessor's productivity.

For business owners employing a large workforce, they should do everything in their power to keep quality employees, regardless of cost.

The way I see it, pay them now…or you will pay later!

On the flip side, let's analyze an employee with a negative attitude along with being that workplace 'cancer.'

You know the ones.

They always view the glass half-empty instead of half-full.

The ones who stir the shit, when it doesn't need stirring.

This kind of behavior can also demonstrate a low level of career mojo!

Frustrated, scorned, and apathetic job seekers who felt like they got screwed over (maybe they did) should be asking themselves "Am I too confrontational?"

Then, there are those individuals who post on social media about a bad work environment and the pitfalls of an organization that lacks quality leadership.

Is that justifiable?

Does it make them feel better about the situation?

Brody is a recent college graduate and works in an advertising sales role that he loathes since it was not his first choice when he earned his Bachelor's in Marketing.

After one year, the comfort seal was broken, and he became a little more confrontational with his manager.

Although he does not call out anyone specifically, he has been putting out discretionary posts on Facebook and humorous videos on Tik Tok to his so-called 'private groups' about working for a shady company with no quality of leadership.

Worse, he begins posting and sharing on LinkedIn referencing how a real leader should be in the workplace.

And it doesn't take long before someone puts two and two together.

But Brody doesn't seem to care, he has interviews lined up with one foot out the door.

Now, we do have freedom of speech which gives us the right to piss, moan, and be a wee bit rebellious at times.

But when it comes to putting out these so-called subliminal messages about what a leader should be, what do you think a hiring manager or third-party investigative workforce solutions firm is going to think about Brody if they start going through his posts on LinkedIn or other social media sites?

I'll tell you.

Brody can potentially be viewed as an office 'cancer.'

The morale is ... it may be wise to keep the negative shit to yourself and off social media if you plan on seeking positions with more reputable companies.

Possessing a track record for outstanding production means little if you are oozing toxicity and fostering a bad culture in the workplace.

Although this next topic is not related to soft skills, I want to allocate some space to discuss it.

Body art.

And the reason is, it can still impede a person's chance of landing that dream job.

From time to time, I get asked by clients about whether they should cover them up for an interview… or let their exterior expressiveness show.

Fifteen years ago, it would have been appalling to see client-facing white-collar professionals displaying tattoos in any form.

Parents would warn their kids " no one will hire you with a tattoo!"

As a former outside sales rep, I have seen co-workers wearing long sleeve shirts on a day where the heat index would climb to 100 degrees, simply because the company's policy called for no noticeable markings on the skin, regardless of whether it was a little mushroom or a large flaming dragon.

Those entering the workforce these days are exteriorly expressing themselves more than any other generation.

Now, many companies centered on high-tech, creative, and entertainment services welcome individuality and an eclectic form of expression and have no issues whatsoever with body art, as long as it is not vulgar, or offensive.

But who determines what is vulgar or offensive?

For example, say an employee in Georgia shows up to work with a brand-new rebel flag permanently stenciled on their forearm.

Will a fellow employee of color take offense to it?

If a new hire has a marijuana leaf predominantly displayed on the back of their neck, in a state where recreational weed is legal. Will someone who is anti-drug in any form be offended?

Or, say an individual earns their LPN certification for a new role at an assisted living center and their neck is covered with tattoos. How would a frail senior citizen take to that?

Occasionally, I have asked my HR clients whether they would consider moving forward with an applicant covered in body art for an office or client-facing role.

Many of them had no issue whatsoever as long as it was done in good taste with no offensive content. Others, had issues if they were located on the face, neck, or fingers.

Not because of their own beliefs, because it was company policy.

Now, this can be looked at in two ways from the candidate's point of view. And both of them would be valid points:

1."Screw them!" "If the company doesn't embrace my body art in any form, I don't want to work for them anyway!"

2. "Will this tattoo impact my chances of getting hired with a reputable firm?

Therefore, if someone asks me what I think, I explain it like this:

If you want that dream job bad enough, consider spending a few bucks and get some concealer (I recommend Dermablend).

How's that for a happy medium?

Another topic I have had to frequently address with my clients over the last several years is drugs…

Particularly marijuana.

With the influx of states (and all of Canada) that are passing rapid legislation to pass it medically and recreationally, more companies are becoming conflicted on whether to test for weed…or not.

In June 2021, Amazon announced that they were ceasing pre-employment marijuana screenings for most job applicants (excluding drivers and heavy equipment operators).

Furthermore, they have reinstated employment eligibility for some former workers and applicants who were fired or had a job offer rescinded for getting busted on a drug test.

To add another nugget in the bowl, Amazon, is also lobbying the federal government to legalize weed.

Now, if you're thinking that they are promoting this to encourage a gummy-chewing, toking culture…or a new product to deliver to your door…

Guess again.

According to their HR department,* it is warranted for two key reasons:

1. Out of necessity to keep up with an increasingly tight labor pool.
2. Combatting the ongoing and disproportionately affected communities of color and minorities and their inequitable treatment.

How's that for embracing diversity!

For all you professionals stuck in a career rut….have you considered switching to the cannabis industry to ease your pain?

Several of my clients have been seeking roles in the cannabis industry but were having a difficult time transitioning their backgrounds and optimizing their skills effectively to align with the needs of this growing vertical to influence a hiring decision-maker.

Each year, it seems that the U.S. is inching closer to federally legalizing weed and with CBD-related products appearing on retail shelves from med spas to gas stations, supply chain & logistics professionals will have their work cut out for them.

How ironic that something that was traditionally scrutinized is now rapidly cultivating?

Whether society embraces it or not, medical and recreational cannabis usage will continue to flourish as more states continue to push decriminalization and legalization through legislation along with a job market that will continue offering opportunities for professionals to pack up their boxes and capitalize on our country's newest cash cow.

If you're a facility manager or team lead working in production, supply chain, or logistics you could showcase your ability to lead projects, new processes, and train warehouse employees. Also, implement quality assurance, safety, and continuous improvement in a fast-paced environment.

Also, how you interact with vendors to ensure supply stock, orders, and deliveries are meeting efficient levels.

For professionals in bioscience and chemistry, you can highlight your experiences working in a laboratory setting along with proficiencies in FDA guidelines and compliances.

Relevant skills in an industry like agribusiness could be

integrating pest management systems to identify and document insects and diseases to maintain plant health or developing treatment strategies within a living soil system.

These could be potential influencers and value-added attributes to an employer at an outdoor growth facility.

As of December 2020, 34 states and the District of Columbia have passed laws that legalize marijuana for medical purposes, with 14 of those states legalizing recreational usage for adults 21 and older.

Despite the economic setbacks from COVID-19, in a recent collaborative study by Leafly and labor consulting firm Whitney Economics, it is estimated that cannabis-related businesses in the US generated over $18.3 billion in annual revenue in 2020 (a 71% increase over 2019) employing over 320,000.*

For jobseekers sniffing around online employment portals, opportunities have been spouting up for master growers, crop consultants, territory managers, laboratory analysts, product formulators, directors of operations, CBD brand ambassadors, quality control & assurance managers, and production supervisors. (Did you think I just meant budtenders?)

Let us not forget ancillary products and services that incorporate device manufacturers, software engineers, security equipment, banking services, and legal professionals fighting for the rights of companies and growers to keep America toking, taking, or applying THC/CBD products.

If you were old enough to remember Cheech & Chong, who would have thought, higher education would have a whole new meaning.

These days, colleges & universities are offering cannabis courses in law, finance, chemistry, agronomy, and botany.

Currently, Northern Michigan University and Minot State University offer a four-year degree in medicinal plant chemistry and the Maryland School of Pharmacy offers a Master's degree in Medical Cannabis Science & Therapeutics requiring only a four-year degree that doesn't have to be centered on science.

For many, migration to professional opportunities in the cannabis industry may still be fleeting, however, as we continue to see more legislators in other states approve outright legalization, companies who can weather an increasingly competitive cannabinoid landscape will be filling open roles, and hiring managers will be interviewing instead of interrogating.

So, if you can get over any personal biases, your future may include greener pastures.

Chapter 3

Confidence and Conviction

Nydia was a highly talented senior-level software engineer who rapidly progressed with an established enterprise solutions firm.

One morning, she and three other team members were told to meet in the conference room.

The looks around the room were unsettling, even though they were told two weeks ago that despite a pending acquisition from a global titan, their department was safe.

Surprise…surprise!

As the severance packets were handed out, a security person was waiting to escort each of them to their cubicles to gather their belongings before walking them out of the office.

And into the world… of the abyss.

After hitting the bar for some day drinking….devastation, confusion, and enragement were followed by insecurity, depression, and hopelessness.

"Why was it us?"

"What did we do wrong?"

These are typical ranges of emotion any of us would feel. So naturally, they are coursing through the minds of Nydia and her jilted team members.

What wasn't revealed to her and the rest of the team, was that during this acquisition, it had already been decided that a third-party overseas software firm was already in place.

The new company had an engineering department that was going to facilitate the current work until that external service took over in the states.

Later, it was leaked out that between the overseas internal department, and the recent hiring of that third-party contractor, it was projected that this move was going to reduce costs in their department by almost 20%.

So, the only thing Nydia and her team were guilty of was a more favorable standard of living!

This can easily mess with anyone's head, especially if they are older and the prospects of finding something close to what they were making can seem dismal.

In many instances where performance was not the issue these circumstances usually circle back to controlling profit & loss, reducing overhead, and ensuring shareholders are still receiving their dividend checks.

But that self-doubt still claws and scratches at Nydia.

What she needs to embrace is that it wasn't her lack of abilities.

In this case, it was either the company's greed, trying to stay competitive, or both.

Other factors that tear at the fiber of the gainfully employed are hard work, dedication, and a consistent level of overachievement that is still not enough for leadership teams to appreciate.

Bryson is a sales rockstar, he is consistently in the top ten percent among his peers in generating revenue and he has cultivated some solid relationships with his key clients who have learned to trust his expertise.

But when co-workers see Bryson, they comment on his demeanor and notice a certain dread in his eyes.

Turns out, although Bryson has consistently exceeded his monthly quotas, and despite his tenacious efforts to continue improving, his manager is constantly up his ass telling him he should be doing better!

Is this motivating Bryson? Or, setting him up for failure?

My guess would be the latter.

Bryson is placed in a very common situation, where his manager lacks the emotional intelligence to properly communicate more effectively with him.

To make matters worse, he opts to look past his award-winning accomplishments, taking the "what have you done for me lately?" stance (Which is typical).

Not to insult anyone's intelligence, but in today's job market, everyone knows that you cannot lead with fear.

Don't they?

This demonstrates ignorance, laziness, and lack of creativity. Also, because they are milking Bryson like a cash cow, they are potentially breeding rebelliousness and insecurity.

This can lead to Bryson exhibiting less effort because, hell, no matter what he does, it is never going to be good enough!

Although Bryson is resilient on the outside and enjoys sales, do we truly know what is going on inside his head?

Will his vulnerabilities start to show and cast doubts about future sales roles with another company?

I mean, God forbid, what will his next manager do if he doesn't perform at an all-star level right out of the gate?

Many of my clients are embarrassed when it comes to their resumés, which is why I have a saying: 'Never call anyone's baby ugly.'

Their confidence level is already dwindling, the last thing I am going to do is agree with them.

Therefore, by turning their obstacles into opportunities, I not only focus on optimizing their background and illustrating what they can contribute to an organization, but through a consultative approach, I am also striving to eliminate any pain points (which I'll discuss in another chapter).

After the resumé is rewritten properly to align and demonstrate how they can contribute to the needs of another employer, I often suggest that they form a 'relationship' with their resumé, embrace change, and keep those wheels turning!

Perhaps I should clarify when I say 'relationship' with the resumé.

Too many times, jobs seekers will throw their resumé on a job board without taking the time to update it with any relevant info (Spray and Pray).

I compare this method to my time in Virginia throwing traps out into the Chesapeake Bay hoping to land some blue crab.

This was a process that took very little effort and after a week or two, I would go back and check the traps.

Many times I ended up with nothing…but I always left them in the same spot.

So, if I wanted those blue crabs bad enough, I probably should have been more diligent in moving my traps to some different spots in the bay during the week.

My point is, if you are aggressively seeking a new position or trying to land that remote dream job, you should be examining your resumé each week!

Also, if any postings that come your way get your juices flowing, it should be worth taking a few minutes to review them and see if any items can be added to your resumé to make more of an impact?

Yes, this can be tedious, but if you are forming that bond with your resumé, this process should become more seamless.

When I say embrace change, I am stating that one standard resumé will simply not cut it for many job seekers in today's competitive market. You may need to tweak it 10 or 20 times.

This also involves changing your thought pattern to focus on a company's requirements versus your previous experiences.

When I work with a client, there are always solid attributes that can be extracted from their background. It's getting them to look at it from a different perspective that can pose the biggest challenge.

Having done that, not only will they feel better about themselves, but they will also be able to convey with confidence and conviction what they can bring to a new position.

And finely tune their career mojo!

As far as those companies Nydia and Bryson worked for? Screw em… it's their loss!

Chapter 4

Predator vs. Prey

As the lioness gazes into the savannah, she comes across a pack of antelope.

Salivating at the sight of the herd, her heart races with anticipation as she coolly maneuvers herself closer and closer to the band.

When the moment strikes, she makes her move aggressively tracking down a slower, older, (and maybe dumber) antelope, clamps down on its jugular, and drags it off into her area of sanctuary for a glorious feast for her and her cubs!

In the wilderness, it's kill or be killed.

Similarly, in a competitive job market, the weak and ignorant might wither and perish...while the strong can persevere and move on.

Pretty grim analogy, eh?

In certain circles, individuals already have their career path nicely paved due to a background of wealth and privilege.

For others, a strong family foundation that is supportive and provides guidance along their educational journey.

Unfortunately for many, a rocky road filled with obstacles and shitty luck.

Regardless of one's circumstance, for the most part, working harder and smarter should always prevail!

If anything, knowing that at least you gave it everything you had should stick with you!

And trust me, others will take notice!

As I mentioned previously, many times you must find a way to create your luck. For me, it took a few years and a stint in the Navy to put things in perspective.

Call it, my moment of clarity!

Basically, it came down to asking myself: "What am going to do with my life?"

I had opportunities but chose to deviate from them. As a result, I had to learn the hard way (which I will go into more detail about in the next chapter).

In a competitive job market, those who strive to aggressively network, accumulate certifications, proactively complete those training & development courses, or finish a degree, are taking the initiative to better themselves mentally and physically.

And this is how you morph into…the predator!

Faith has always been passionate about teaching. Call it a labor of love, but she has always been committed to molding young minds.

Over time, she realizes that if she wants to take her career to the next level as an administrator, she needs to look at the big picture which means developing professionally on her own time.

Even with a supportive husband and three kids heavily involved in extra-curricular activities.

So, for the next three years, she immerses herself in online courses, earns an MBA in education, in addition to completing certifications to enhance her administrative and leadership abilities.

Furthermore, she gets more involved with organizations and volunteers for community service.

Fortunately, her superiors take notice, and she begins filling in as assistant principal when needed.

Now, Faith has positioned herself for the next level in her career!

Did some obstacles get in her way, like being an inattentive mom and wife at times?

Most likely…

However, this positive shift in her career can now provide more opportunities for her family.

Instead of waiting for something to fall in her lap, she has made herself more marketable, and in doing so, positioned herself as a predator instead of being the prey.

And that is called…a personal investment!

It's no secret that I always encourage my clients to take a predator approach instead of waiting for something to drop out of the sky.

This is even more critical for those seeking a career change!

It always baffles me that many individuals who are looking to get into a new role stick with only one job board.

Did they ever consider all those job postings they are missing out on?

Also, did they consider the slew of job boards that employers have to choose from?

What if that company decides not to post an opening on a particular site?

Even if they hire a service to scatter them out to say 50+ employment sites…how long are they going to be prominent?

For example, although anyone can post a job on Indeed for free, these 'organic' postings lose visibility over time, so, unless they pony up some funds to promote a 'sponsored job' they are not going to be as effective in boosting a job seeker's interest.

There is, however, one search engine that will make hunting for any role or even those you didn't even know you were looking for, more seamless.

I call it the mothership of job boards.

Google.

Type in any job search in a particular market or simply make up something and see what pops up. Just add the word 'job' along with it.

For example Environmental Project Coordinator remote **jobs** in Kissimmee, FL.

You never know what you might find.

How much bullshit is a person willing to take in the workplace?

One of the main drivers that propel individuals to seek out new opportunities is their threshold for showing up for another helping of it each day.

Many times, we put up with more crap than necessary because of family obligations like paying for college, a medical condition that requires a decent health plan, or the golden paycheck that is too enticing to walk away from.

This says a lot about the character of that person because they are sacrificing their happiness and contentment for the greater good of their family.

Many times, it is a team effort as both spouses work doing what it takes to get it done!

However, there is also the risk of being complacent.

We are used to routines where we have developed a comfort zone.

Over the years, I have worked with senior employees and high-level executives at Caterpillar, John Deere, Nestlé, Boeing, Microsoft, Federal agencies, and many other global enterprises, local businesses, and companies.

These are individuals who have been employed there for 25 years and more but are not able to retire just yet.

And something else...

They were all apprehensive, nervous, and tentative about moving on regardless of who's decision it was.

It's natural.

That's why I have deemed this as being institutionalized.

Have you ever seen The Shawshank Redemption?

There is a clip in the movie where an inmate is granted parole after serving 50 years.

During his stretch, he becomes the prison librarian which doesn't amount to much since he just pushes a cart of books around while deceptively smuggling small pieces of forbidden contraband for packs of cigarettes.

However, in the joint, he is a man of influence and respect, with keen prison acumen (kind of an oxymoron isn't it).

For many years he has had the same routine, he loads up the books and magazines in his cart and marks everything down on his clipboard.

As he stated…

Easy Peasy!

By the time his parole was granted, he is old, arthritic, and petrified!

He even goes so far as to take a blade to the throat of a fellow inmate in hopes they would let him stay inside Shawshank!

When he finally gets out, he discovers a world of radical change.

He transitions to a halfway house and takes a job bagging groceries, but all he thinks about is going back to Shawshank.

Unfortunately, the story tragically ends with him hanging himself in his one-room domicile.

Like the lion and the antelope, this scenario is equally grim, however, this time, I am stressing this lack of receptiveness and fear to change.

Simply put, we need comfort, security, and a little peace of mind.

Even if the day is so bad it drives us to the brink of insanity.

It's common to say: That's it, I'm getting my resumé in order!"

Many times, it is reactionary.

Therefore, it's typical for me to do a resumé for a client, only to discover a year later, that they are still doing the same thing, with little effort for finding something new.

Unless you lived in a monastery in some remote outpost it's common to have some employees who collectively rendezvous at lunchtime and at after-work get-togethers to piss and moan about a boss, a supervisor, a co-worker who gets treated more favorably, and how unfair they are being treated.

This is the therapy and the tonic needed to make it through another week.

Believe me, I totally get it!

Because I for one, dread change as well!

More than the average person, I will say.

My wife will tell you that I am all about routine and I do not like to deviate from it!

From 2001 to 2017 I stuck it out with only two companies. According to the U.S. Bureau of Labor Statistics in 2021, the average longevity of employment with one company was 4.1 years. To drill it down, the median tenure for ages 25 to 34 was 2.8 years.*

Speaking from personnel experience, my reason for radical change stems from the predator mentality that sooner or later I was going to meet my fate professionally. So I decided to proactively move forward on my own terms to ensure my survival.

Was I scared and apprehensive?

Hell yes!

But I had finally had enough.

To take it a step further, one year after I launched Resumedics in Peoria, IL, I opened a second location in Colorado Springs, CO!

What the hell was wrong with me?

I'll tell you….

A rolling stone gathers no moss!

Now, I'm going to part with several secrets throughout this book…

The first…is my lack of respect for authority that goes as far back as my military days.

Oh, I worked hard and performed well, but many of my

former bosses will concur that I was a 'Maverick,' someone who was always looking to do it differently and did not agree with the direction or instructions they outlined.

Looking back, a piece of it was due to my lack of filtering from an untreated condition, (which I will go into more detail about later in this book).

But for the most part, I was always transparent, a realist, which meant I told it like it was and never kissed anyone's ass!

Also, I understand how frustrating it is working for someone who has no leadership qualities.

It's like the blind leading the blind, but you still have to play nice in that sandbox.

If I was a manager… would I want me as an employee?

Probably not….

Not because of performance, I was always a workhorse giving 110 percent, but that came at a price…

I was a pain in the ass!

Fortunately, I had the drive to do something about it before it was too late.

And I have had no regrets!

I think Satchel Page, one of the greatest pitchers of all time said it best…

"Don't look back. Something might be gaining on you!"

Chapter Five

Thank You For Your Service

When I enrolled at Bradley University at the ripe old age of 26, I was always referred to as a 'non-traditional' student.

And I cringed every time I heard that!

Because I was not enrolled as an 18-year-old freshman, that made me non-traditional? (I'm sure this was my insecurity talking).

Utilizing the G.I. Bill, higher education grants, and student loans this 'nowhere man' with little vision finally earned a Bachelor's degree in Communications in 1995...and I ventured out into the job world!

Now, I am not going to sugarcoat this, I thought being a veteran and having that on my resumé would position me above other job candidates and move me to the front of the line.

After all, I served my country honorable and earned a BS.

I was entitled…right?
Wrong!

You see, I was a former Operations Intelligence Specialist with a degree in Public Relations.

Although it sounded distinguished, it was not exactly a matrix for making me marketable for advertising and marketing/communication roles…and here are a few reasons why:

-   I was not trained in graphic design.
-   My internship was with a non-profit instead of an agency.
-   Peoria was not Chicago, so my options were limited.

More importantly, my resumé was simply not aligned with these types of positions. And what was deflating to MY career mojo, was that I couldn't even get a job selling AM radio spots!

At that point in my life, my self-esteem was at its lowest point and I was kicking myself in the ass for pissing away the last three years in college, while my buddies were making twice as much working in the trades!

Finally, after two years of doing waiter & bartending gigs, I landed something, although it wasn't even close to what I went to school for, and it was the shittest job I ever had as a professional (I'll leave it at that).

Looking back, I wish there were more support services to help this vet transition into the civilian job sector more effectively.

Over the years, I have had the honor of working with a diverse group of military members ranging from aeronautical engineers, paint chippers, executive officers, to the frontline grunt soldier.

Now, you would think that those who were more advanced

in their military career would have an easier time transitioning into civilian roles.

But I have found that this is not always the case.

Before I dig deeper into these transitional issues, I did find that in a survey from CareerBuilder.com 48% percent of employers paid more attention to applications submitted by U.S. veterans.*

In addition, 68% of employers said if they had two equally qualified candidates for a job, and one of them was a U.S. veteran, they were more likely to hire the vet.*

But what kind of a job are we talking about here?

Furthermore, this study concluded that while veteran hiring initiatives have gained momentum, approximately two in five veterans still felt like they were underemployed or working in a low-paying job.*

For many vets and active-duty members, military-to-civilian transitioning can be a real struggle.

And for those 'lifers' with longer service times or military-centric job functions, the adjustment could be even harder.

I mean, how many opportunities are there for a torpedo control technician, signalman, or a parachute packer on Indeed?

When I conduct seminars for vets and service members ready to be discharged, I ask them **not to dwell too much on their daily military functions.**

Instead, their focus should be on what they did in the military and how their background is going to **relate to civilian roles!**

So, whether they led an elite force through a hostile village in Iraq, provided mobile readiness for immediate deployment, or ensured that communications and technology infrastructures were maintained, they can still parlay these experiences for civilian jobs in these industries:

- Inventory Management, Supply Chain, and Logistics
- Warehousing, Transportation, and Distribution
- Safety Management and Human Resources
- Employee Training and Development
- Security Services
- Information Technology and Cybersecurity
- Facilities and Food Service Management
- Aviation and Avionics

Some transferable skills can include:

- Critical Decision Making and Analytical Problem Solving
- Process & Continuous Improvement
- Handling High Pressure, Fast-Paced Situations
- Supervising, Teamwork, and Empowering & Motivating Individuals
- HAZMAT and Environmental Health Measures

After spending 12 years in the Army, Devon went back to school to finish his degree in Management Information Systems.

He had been sending out his resumé and to his dismay, he was not getting any responses and more importantly, no qualifiable feedback from academic advisors or transition specialists.

Now, Devon is starting to feel dejected... from being rejected!

During his military career, he had led units consisting of approximately 40 soldiers and oversaw over $20 million worth of high-tech equipment.

After reviewing Devon's resumé, I examined what the functions and qualifications of an entry-level MIS position were and began weaving his relevant (Army) skills into his (MIS) coursework that included:

- Cybersecurity Data (MIS)
- Understanding of Processing (Army)
- Problem Solving (Army)
- Being Detail-Oriented (Army)
- Data Flow Management (MIS)
- Legal & Regulatory Policies (Army & MIS)
- Microsoft Office (MIS & Army)
- Resource Management (MIS & Army)

Now, he will stand a better chance of penetrating applicant tracking screenings (including usajobs.gov).

More importantly, this will strengthen his interviews because he is beginning to adapt to how his past experiences can work with his newly acquired skills.

Personally speaking, when it comes to hiring, I feel that the millions of men and women who served deserve the privilege to be moved to the front of the line!

Unfortunately for many vets, nothing is a given in the civilian job market.

Shannon, a recently retired vet, has spent 22 years in the Navy working in Personnel Administration and Human Resources.

She achieved the rank of Master Chief (E-9) overseeing a department consisting of 35 enlisted staff members. During this period, she also worked at a local recruiting station.

After retiring from active duty, she tried to land several HR jobs, and much to her dismay, her resumé was consistently being rejected.

Furthermore, she was not advancing in any of the interviews she did manage to get.

Perplexed and aggravated, she just couldn't figure out why her years of supervisory experiences could not even land her an entry-level HR gig!

After I reviewed her resumé, I noticed that her experiences were laid out like it was taken right off the Military Occupational Specialty Code:

- Performed annual evaluation details from the processing, coordination of requests, as well as responding to inquiries of evaluations when one party does not agree with performance grades received.

- Worked with soldiers who were eligible for promotion and arranged the promotion ceremony with the Chain of Command.

- Evaluated soldiers' career desires and qualifications for advanced assignments and prepared and processed requests for transfer or reassignment and processed classification, discharge, or reclassification actions.

- Processed and executed Personnel Service Center SIDPERS level procedures and actions.

Now, do you think a hiring decision-maker is going to invest a substantial amount of time deciphering that?

After some 'civilianizing' of her experiences, I came up with something that jived a little better for private sector HR gigs:

- Collaborated with senior management regarding the annual performance evaluations of personnel and initiated corrective action plans to assist in their professional development to higher levels of responsibility.

- Coordinated travel arrangements and logistics globally utilizing proprietary systems to ensure a smooth transition to worldwide destinations.

- Led event planning for ongoing ceremonies that consisted of partnering with cross-functional teams for submitting and receiving plaques and setting up accommodations for incoming dignitaries.

- Implemented new information systems to streamline HR processes including benefits and payroll, while updating policies and procedures affecting over 2,500 personnel.

Additional skills that I added to her resumé included:
- Data Entry and Employee Recordkeeping
- Onboarding and Exit Strategies
- Employee Development Programs
- Talent Acquisition and Recruiting

Just like any promotion, you still need to demonstrate why you are deserving.

If I was qualified to be a behavior counselor, I would go into more detail regarding another unfortunate scenario that has affected too many military personnel…

Post-Traumatic Stress Disorder (PTSD).

Although veterans are usually associated with this condition, many professionals like firefighters and law enforcement can also be impacted by this.

As I was doing more research on PTSD, I discovered a collaboration on an essay done by George A. Bonanno, a professor of clinical psychology at Columbia Teachers College, and Meghan Mobbs, a Ph.D. student, and former U.S. Army officer entitled, 'Beyond War and PTSD.' *

I found this to be an insightful piece because it talks about something that probably occurs more than PTSD:

Transition Stress.

Here's the foundation:

Throughout one's military career, service members are achieving a sense of purpose that can include well-defined roles, hierarchy, camaraderie, and honor.*

When they transition out of the military and into private sector roles these characteristics can be harder to define.*

Consequently, this can result in a loss of identity and regardless of pay grade, become very challenging to deal with.

Picture going from being a member of the world's most elite workforce to spiraling down to an entry-level capacity.

It would be easy to see why this could bring on symptoms like anxiety, depression, and other behavioral issues.

These signals could also breed major relational and professional conflicts in the workplace!

And take that career mojo down to a whole new level!

As I stated previously, I'm not a psychologist, I just deal with career transition. However, I still feel a sense of responsibility to be as completely transparent when I consult with any member of the Armed Forces.

Reflecting on my military career, I certainly wasn't a poster boy for exemplary service during my four years in the Navy.

Hopefully, by continuing to help other vets, one day, I'll be 'square with the house.' so to speak.

I guess time will tell.

Chapter Six

The Battle of the Bots

For you old-timers back in the nineties, remember when resumé paper quality and a slick-looking template could still woo a hiring decision-maker?

And your choice in distributing it was the regular mail, dropping it off in person, faxing, or emailing.

These were the simpler times when things made more sense.

Then, the digital age swooped it, and natural language processing, data mining, algorithms, and omnichannel talent acquisition began taking over.

Job boards like Indeed, ZipRecruiter, and LinkedIn are now your partner in the wonderful world of job searching, thus, ushering in…

The resumé robot!

Emotionless, apathetic, and with warp speed, these highly advanced systems screen a resumé in a millisecond before calculating a score.

If it scores high enough…then it moves on to a human set of eyes for another glace over.

Just like an onion, the initial hiring process begins with peeling back the layers.

The technical term is applicant tracking system (ATS) and it has been a progressive thorn in the side of billions of job seekers for over 20 years!

In an interesting 2019 study from Preptel (a candidate optimization/job search service), they estimated that 75% of all resumés are never even seen by a human set of eyes!*

According to cleaverism.com, there are roughly 60 ATS platforms that are prevalent in the marketplace today* and CNBC reported that 95% of all Fortune 500 companies are using these systems.*

And they all seem to have their idiosyncrasies.

Now, I can give you facts, theories, or just my two cents on how these digital creatures decide what resumés go on through…or trigger an auto rejection email.

So, let's start with facts:

ATS filters a resumé automatically by utilizing criteria such as keywords, skills, employment experience, and education before reaching a living, breathing decision-maker.

That is all I say with the utmost conviction.

Although I can see where this platform can relieve some of the tediousness of reviewing tons of resumés, it's my contention that by taking the human element out of the initial screening of a qualified candidate, companies are losing out on acquiring some outstanding talent.

And job seekers are shaking their heads wondering why their resumés are not penetrating the automated 'gatekeeper.'

When I started drilling down into all the different ATS software and the recommendations for effectively penetrating them, I too was frustrated by all the different guidelines and answers I was reading from the 'so-called experts.'

And after muddling through these, I deducted that no one seems to know what the hell they are talking about....

Expect promoting THEIR services!

Some say you can use this... some say you can use that..some say templates will work...while others contradict that statement!

Now, how is that supposed to help a job seeker?

Over the last several years, I have consulted with many HR and hiring managers utilizing two of the world's most widely used human resource information systems (HRIS): Workday and Taleo.

By soaking up their input with maximum absorbency, I have developed a system to navigate through the technological madness to pass on to you in the most simplified manner I could think of.

And here it is, (drum roll please!):

First thing, *do your homework!*

As I mentioned in the first chapter, these companies are giving you the answers to the test! Just read through their requirements instead of skimming through them.

Don't assume a robot is going to know that your job title and functions are going to suffice.

Second thing, *does any of your skills and background align with the functions of the position you are interested in?*

If you are just sending out the same resumé to tons of job postings, the probability that you are going to get the response you are looking for will be disappointing.

Finally, if you plan to submit your resumé as an attachment through a job portal, I highly recommend *getting rid of any templated formats.*

Items that many job seekers typically have on a templated resumé include page footers, reverse panels, icons, logos, photos, multiple columns, text boxes, and excessive lines across the page.

These things can potentially throw the algorithms off ATS screenings (generating those auto rejection emails).

In a competitive job market, individuals are not going to earn creative style points on their resumé....content is the key driver!

Also, copying and pasting a job posting verbatim is NOT something I recommend.

What is acceptable is taking keywords from these descriptions and using them on your resumé.

Don't worry if you don't meet every single criterion, because if you did, we could just call it plagiarism and move on (and we don't want to do that).

When I design a resumé for my client, I always ensure it is *keyword optimized for specific roles* and can *pernitrate ATS software.*

With that in mind, I use Microsoft Word only, regular bullets, and no underlines or italics. I do, however, like bold typing keywords and using small vertical lines to separate skills.

Also, the content should read easily left to right and top to bottom.

And don't be afraid to use the whole page! Having too much white space will just lead to creating unnecessary pages.

Finally, don't jump off a cliff if your resumé is more than one page.

In the digital age, no one cares!

For you creative folks (graphic designers especially) who like some flair, keep in mind that an infographic style may have a hard time penetrating ATS.

If someone wants to view a portfolio of your work, consider adding a URL link at the top of your resumé.

Now, just because a resumé needs to be content-driven, there can still be a happy medium when it comes to style.

My favorite fonts are Garamond 11 point and Century Gothic 10 point, both convey a modern, professional look, that is easy on the eyes and still rank extremely high for ATS compatibility.

Another important factor is making sure your resumé is easy to import on job site portals. When you start spending half a day importing an infographic format, you'll get the point.

Strategically speaking, many job seekers I initially consult with try and put everything they can into one resumé.

I call this 'cramming and jamming.'

Unfortunately, they also receive a lot of rejection emails because they lose sight of specific elements that might weigh heavily during the ATS screening process.

If I had to guestimate the percentage of clients that I have worked with that are familiar with the term ATS…yet have no understanding of how it works, I would put it at 50%.

Which is a shame.

Companies like Indeed, ZipRecruiter, and CareerBuilder spend millions on advertising their platforms painting a picture of success stories for individuals.

You know the ones.

One second, the working mom receives her degree, next, she is shaking hands with the hiring manager, then a big thumbs up!

What they leave out is the integrated element that needs to go into these resumés.

By now you may be thinking, "What the hell is that?"

Think about it like this…

Just because you jammed a bunch of keywords into your resumé…are you examining how your work background aligns with these roles?

How is this going to come off in an interview when someone asks you to walk them through your resumé?

I preach this time and time again; you will get a much better response by tailoring your resumé for specific jobs.

If you just throw it up on a job site and hope for the best, you may be waiting a long time before you get the desired response.

Remember, be the predator and do not depend on the Spray and Pray method!

Not only can ATS systems be finicky, but where does someone start first when they read any manuscript?

At the top!

So, the capabilities you can bring to new roles can be highlighted with a strong SUMMARY OF QUALIFICATIONS or PROFILE at the top of the resumé to provide relevancy to those positions.

Question: Do you know what the average time a hiring manager initially spends on a resumé is?

Six to ten seconds!

And they always start at the top. Therefore, the SUMMARY should be the most important part of the resumé, so it needs to make an impact!

Did you know that the word resumé derives from the French word: résumé.

This means... ***to summarize.***

Your summary should focus on how YOUR qualifications ALIGN with the COMPANY'S requirements for that position(s).

Now, it can be tempting to use this to pile on your achievements and accolades, but that should be saved for your work history.

This is not a bio!

Here is an example of a Before and After summary for a senior-level software engineer seeking a higher-level management role.

BEFORE
- Extensive expertise in managing teams, processes, and strategic programs for cross-functional initiatives, projects, compliances, operational processes, and procedures within corporate guidelines.

- Adept at communicating and collaborating with engineers, customer service, project managers, and operations teams, to design new processes, meet service goals and realize continuous improvement.

- Recognized as a high performer with a focus on delivering excellence.

AFTER

- Data-centric, software engineering manager with over 10 years of project leadership experience empowering high-performing technology teams to deliver enterprise solutions using best practices.

- Recognized for innovations in structural design, product ownership, and continuous improvement in ever-changing technology landscapes utilizing Agile methodologies, critical thinking, and qualitative problem-solving.

- Employs influential communication techniques to motivate and train developers globally, while fostering a positive workplace culture in a start-up or matrixed environment.

- Collaborates effectively with cross-functional teams and vendors and presents complex metrics to executives, key stakeholders, and customers.

After reviewing both summaries, the rewritten one is now conveying what this software engineer can contribute to a high-tech firm by properly utilizing definitive keywords.

Many hiring managers and recruiters have also told me they prefer to see the skills separately at the top of the resumé so they know what a candidate can utilize instead of being buried at the bottom.

Think about it…if the resumé sucks… they may not even get to the bottom of it!

Here are some suggested keywords and skills that can help this software engineer:
- Scrum
- Software Development Lifecycle (SDLC)
- Integrated Messaging
- Cloud Migration
- Data Analytics
- Automated Testing and Validation
- Quality Assurance
- KPI Reporting
- Network Security
- Sprint Planning
- Human Capital Management
- Domain-Driven Design (DDD)
- Virtual Meetings

Another critical element is substantiating the summary and skills throughout the work history. Doing this will also be boosting the ATS score.

As far as work history goes, this is the area where having too much or too little information can make a message hard to interpret.

Even if your resumé passes ATS, the majority of hiring managers may still only spend less than 10 seconds scanning it.

Therefore, I advocate a clear and concise sentence structure.

Also ask yourself: "How relevant is this information?" Do I need to put what I did 20 years ago on it?

Another key driver that can set a candidate apart is more detail on projects, programs, and performance metrics.

Do not assume that an extensive description of daily functions is going to translate to a new job posting since you don't know how technical, creative, or innovative the initial decision-maker is?

In other words… you may have to 'dumb it down.'

For many job seekers, copying and pasting their job descriptions may be the easiest and most time-efficient route to go.

The only problem is… many individuals will do that verbatim… without any modifications whatsoever.

Consider this…

What if the person who wrote that job description sucks at writing?

While Indeed, LinkedIn, CareerBuilder, and ZipRecruiter are the heavy hitters in the resumé/job hunting industry, here are some items of interest:

Importing your information onto their templates is fine if you are only submitting them through THEIR job board.

So, if you are using Indeed's template, it may not have the same effect if you elect to run it through ZipRecruiter's portal.

Also, these templated resumés should not be the only style you use.

If given the option to import a Word Doc or PDF into a company's internal job portal, I suggest going that route.

Conquering the 'bots' is very attainable...you just need some extra diligence.

And if you are not a fan of ATS...then tough shit.

They are here to stay!

Chapter 7

Overcoming Pain Points

For many homeowners, fixing, upgrading, or installing items around the house is commonplace.

Sometimes, it's all about aesthetics, other times, a situation that needs immediate attention.

One summer, we had a ceiling fan break down. It was 20 years old and served its purpose.

As I trucked on down to Lowe's to purchase a new one, I had assured my wife that installing it would be a breeze (no pun intended).

With the help of my buddy, (who was not a professional electrician) removing the old fan was no problem, and I made sure that I knew what wires went where.

However, after spending an entire afternoon trying to install the new one, I finally bit the bullet and call an electrician who specialized in ceiling fans of all shapes and sizes to come out and finish the job.

He had it properly assembled, balanced, and running in 30 minutes!

By this time, you might be wondering where I am going with this story, and how does it relate to writing a resumé?

Well, for many do-it-yourselfers, they soon discover that creating a resumé and cover letter to transition careers can be a real pain in the ass and extremely time-consuming!

And the first step in this process is usually incorporating the assistance of a friend, spouse, or co-worker.

After all, it's just typing up information, right?

Sometimes they are successful...other times, not so much.

Now, if everyone was a master wordsmith, content influencer, keyword optimizing guru, or a 'career engineer' there would be no need for services like mine.

Even I struggle with content... like trying to make this book more interesting!

Whether it's a termination, being put on a performance plan, demotion, miserable work environment, or proactively seeing what your value is in the market, some job seekers are going to be faced with many pain points as they begin the process of getting their resumé in order.

If you are a mid to executive-level professional working on your resumé...Do any of these scenarios apply to you?

- Wrestling with how to consolidate years of diverse experiences into a clear and concise format?
- Not getting the feedback you were hoping for from other companies?
- Frustrated with all the different opinions about keywords and applicant tracking systems (ATS)?
- Seeking a 'returnship' back into the workforce and you need to explain some work gaps?

Now, I'm about to part with another little secret....

Potential employers don't care diddly about your employment background.

Stay with me on this one.

Copying and pasting a job function on a resumé does not take much creativity.

However, I see it constantly.

To be effective and create excitement, a great resumé helps the hiring decision-maker envision YOU delivering similar achievements at THEIR company.

And that means making sure your background jives with their requirements in some capacity.

With a little bit of diligence, you may be surprised how your qualifications align with that company's roles, vision, and mission.

There is nothing wrong with being a go-getting, problem solving, people person...but that pretty much sums up 99% of the candidate pool, don't you think?

Recently, I conducted a survey on LinkedIn to find out what the biggest pain point was when it came to writing a resumé.

1. ATS formatting.
2. Modifying it for different jobs.
3. Too many rejections.
4. Consolidating work history.

Over 80% of those polled stated that modifying it for different jobs was their biggest struggle.

Thanks to COVID-19 the trajectory of how certain industries are doing business has been altered.

There is also a workforce attached to these verticals that are discovering that they might need to pivot to new opportunities, because of the challenges they are facing.

Think about a company that specializes in selling office furniture.

With more people working from home, what kind of demand is there for new, ergonomic accessories for an office complex?

Now, think about a company that manufacturer sheds.

Not the ones you store the lawnmower and garden tools in.

I'm talking about those little buildings that can be constructed in the backyard, fully equipped with electricity, and capable of providing all the amenities of an office.

Do you want to know what these two companies have in common?

A shifting workforce.

Business to business (B2B) account managers who were aggressively prospecting for new clients to market office furniture (B2B) could migrate to marketing sheds to a new demographic; business to consumer (B2C).

Here are some other examples of how changes in one industry can influence professionals to pivot into new ones.

Relators who face the prospects of having minimal listings due to a housing shortage can look to opportunities in property management by using their ability to close contracts, negotiate, and sell to a diverse market.

How about educators who are burned out from dealing with new protocols being forced upon them that impede their ability to teach students?

They could potentially integrate curriculum development, lesson planning, and educational software implementation for marketing technology platforms to schools or parlay that into training & development positions.

For the last eight years, Morgan has been working as an advertising account manager for a large daily newspaper.

The key revenue driver has always been the print product, however, during this period, that product has rapidly eroded going from a circulation of almost 50,000 down to 18,000.

To combat this decline, she has been marketing a smorgasbord of multimedia products (print and online) to her book of business and new clients.

Overall, she likes selling online advertising. This allows her to showcase her creativity and offer new solutions to her clients earning their trust and respect.

However, she sees the writing on the wall and realizes that to continue thriving in online advertising she will have to seek opportunities elsewhere.

She was sending her resumé out to several digital marketing firms, but she was not getting very far.

Once I reviewed it, I noticed something quite glaring.

Morgan was positioning herself primarily as a seller of print advertising with a passion for marketing online products as well.

So, the first thing I suggested was that she reverse her behavioral pattern.

Instead of viewing herself as a marketer of print advertising with a passion for online advertising, she **rebrands** herself as an **online specialist** and minimizes the print component (or eliminates it).

The common theme individuals gravitate to… is listing everything they do in their work history!

For whatever reason, by not coming clean about every job function they worry about misrepresenting themselves.

In Morgan's case, the digital firms are not going to give a shit about how much she sold in print. They want to know about her accomplishments selling newspaper.com ads, analyzing performance metrics and successfully targeting demographics for social media campaigns.

Fortunately, these are items that she has a demonstrated track record of excelling in…even if it's with a newspaper conglomerate.

So, her new keywords should focus on lead & demand generation, hyper-targeted demographics, SEO conversions, engagement, and ROI. All of these are vital components in digital advertising.

Also, many individuals overthink their job titles.

One company might use the title of a sales position as Account Executive, another company may use Territory Sales Manager.

Both can mean the same thing with no supervisory experience.

Therefore, Morgan can brand herself as a Multimedia Consultant, and she would not be fabricating anything!

Another major pain point that is a driving force in dismantling career mojo is the interview process.

As I mentioned in the first chapter, some are just better at bullshitting.

What I didn't mention was that others are simply better at preparing for them.

But, what about those who just fumble and freeze up trying to find the right words...or, always find themselves in a dilemma involving that long pause when trying to answer a question?

One of the most common behavioral interviewing methods employers use is STAR (Situation, Task, Action, Result).

Here is a quick breakdown of what the interviewer may ask a candidate using this process:

Situation:

Describe something they found themselves involved with?

Task:

What they were required to achieve from the situation?

Action:

What did they execute and why?

Results:

What was the outcome achieved through their actions?

As a certified interview coach, I work with identifying and preparing potential questions for my clients.

More importantly, regardless of the industry, I always like to offer some 'pre-interview' tips:

Carefully review the position you are applying to:

If you are interested in the job, consider going back to the posting and familiarizing yourself with the daily functions and what they are looking for as a quick refresh right before the interview.

Think about how you would answer the question: ***"Describe something challenging and how did you overcome it?"***

After you review THEIR job description, try thinking of something that could relate to the position itself and practice conveying it.

Typically, companies are looking for something that has relevance to their requirements and mission.

Research the organization AND the hiring manager:

Check out employee reviews on a site like Glassdoor to see how they rate. Also, go on LinkedIn and see if there is a profile of that person you can review.

By doing this you might make a potential connection. (They are probably doing it on you, so it's okay to check them out as well, it's not stalking).

You would be surprised what you can learn about hiring decision-makers based on their LinkedIn profile.

I also like to preach three core impacts:
1. The value you can bring to the role.
2. How you will complement their workplace culture.
3. Your Likeability.

Have you ever heard of any advanced degrees in Interviewing?

Neither have I.

Unless you are an HR professional with an extensive background in interviewing, many managers/directors will concur that hiring and firing are some of the most challenging tasks they face.

And it's a role they certainly do not embrace, however, they are still required to be a major piece of the hiring puzzle.

I bring this up because many job seekers think the reason a company didn't proceed further in the hiring process is that they bombed their interview.

What they didn't realize is that sometimes *interviewing* is a challenge for the *interviewer.*

I know that would be extremely frustrating, unfortunately, a common occurrence job seekers are not aware of.

Another question I often get asked is how many pages should the resumé be?

It's not uncommon for me to receive four and five pages of information from my clients (CVs and resumés) and I find that half of it…is repetitiveness and fluff!

And no hiring decision-maker likes fluff!

Let me ask you this… if you are a seasoned professional with years of qualifications, experience, achievements, projects, awards, and performance metrics…

How are you going to cram all of that on one page?

Are you going to use a font so small, you need a high-powered lens to read it? Keep in mind any size font under eight-point may not penetrate an ATS.

These days, a resumé will probably be viewed on a device before it is printed out so two pages are fine…and don't be afraid of using the whole page, also a 10 to 12 point font is the suggested size for the body of your resumé content, (your name can be featured in larger font).

So, here is a quick rule of thumb…Unless you are a recent college graduate or an entry-level professional with not a lot of work history to showcase… a one-pager is fine.

However, if you are a mid to executive-level professional, two pages max is the norm.

This also sets a parameter to ensure your content speaks to the role you are applying to and is tight, concise, very impactful...and reduces any fluff and repetitiveness.

Also, unless it is relevant, many hiring managers only care about the last 10 to 15 years of work history anyway, (especially in an ever-evolving industry like technology) so you can either keep that to a minimum or eliminate those experiences.

There are some exceptions, however...

If you are a doctor, research scientist, Ph.D., tenured college professor, or a professional that has publications, patents, and presentations relevant to what a company is looking for, a third or fourth page will be acceptable.

Also, federal and government roles requiring you to submit a resumé through *usajobs.gov* are going to be more descriptive and these usually need to be four to five pages long. (Which is absurd in my opinion).

So, for those of you hell-bent on a one-page resumé to give to someone, consider using both sides of the page and save a tree!

Naturally, many of us attempt to do certain tasks ourselves, and sometimes it's a little deflating when we finally turn to other options.

What you should ask yourself is...

How much time are you going to invest trying to write and modify a resumé effectively, with no guarantee it will even land you one single interview?

Think about it like this:

If you had a chance to make $5,000 more a year, and all it cost you was $300...

Wouldn't that be a nice return on investment?

If you were an average golfer striving to get better, yet your foursome typically included the same hackers every weekend… would you look to them to improve your game?

Or, perhaps, enlist the help of a golf pro?

If you want to be that 'do-it-yourselfer' with your resumé, may I suggest taking some extra time in examining its contents:

- Does it paint you as a doer instead of an achiever?
- Does it portray you a results-driven?
- Does it illustrate what you have accomplished?

See, it doesn't have to be so painful.

Chapter Eight

Older The Fruit, Sweeter the Juice

Where does the time go?

For you Baby Boomers and Gen X professionals, age discrimination can be very prevalent in today's workforce.
Think about it?
Does a company want to hire a 50+ professional?
Yes and no.

Something resonated with me from an online article I read from Paul Rupert, of Respectful Exits.* He suggests that the predominant business model in the US is still an industrial one where companies view employees as 'human capital.' *

He further elaborates, "companies view their workforce the same way they view their capital equipment....you buy it, you assume it has a certain shelf life, and then you get rid of it and replace it with a new model."*

But what if that 'model' remains diligent on preventative maintenance, stays finely tuned, and well-oiled?

If it is a quality model, it can last many more years and still serve as a highly productive, cost-effective cog in the workforce. Right?

Now, if you fall in that 50+ age range, ask yourself these questions:

- Are you still performing at a higher level than your peers?
- Do you still successfully demonstrate a 'hunter-mentality?
- Are you continuing to build outstanding customer relationships with key decision-makers who value your expertise and years of experience?
- Are you staying up to date with the latest technology?

Now, if you say yes to any of these (or better yet, all of them)…that's all an employer should care about!

Mary, a senior-level product marketing director is 57 years old and still a gamer!

She competes in 10Ks, does her PiYo and Peloton®, has a tremendous work ethic, and leads by example as a nurturing mentor to junior team members in her department.

More importantly, she has proactively improved her proficiencies with some of the latest technology and software platforms, artificial intelligence, and data science for lead and demand generation.

By staying current with the innovative global product lifecycle she has significantly contributed to the company as it continues to generate millions of dollars annually.

She has been with her firm for 12 years, and she shows no signs of slowing down.

Do you think Mary's age is a liability?

For those of you who have been loyal to one company, worked with outdated infrastructure, or have seemed to have slipped through the cracks over the last several years…your future may contain some obstacles.

Andrew is 56 and has played an integral role in his company's rise from a start-up to a national leader in agricultural equipment.

Having 20 years invested with the company, he had risen to the position of VP of Marketing & Communications overseeing a team of 20 associates and was accountable for an annual marketing budget of $1.2 million.

Although he has always been recognized as a brilliant communication strategist and storyteller, pivoting into the digital age was not a strength of Andrew's.

He is well-known for his concepts and leadership but leaves social media management, SEO strategies, and hyper-targeted demand generation to those who work under him or farm it out to third-party vendors.

Last year, his company began a huge merger with a global manufacturer, and Andrew had to interview for his position and try to retain…and justify his $225k salary and seven weeks of vacation he used annually.

When asked about his vision for new product launches and the cutting-edge methods for market growth, he offered very little insight into digital strategies and mobile applications.

He also struggled when asked about elevating user experiences and action plans for influencing the next generation of purchasing decision-makers which were going to be key drivers in marketing these innovative products in a highly competitive global market.

As the merger progressed, Andrew was offered to stay on as a temporary consultant during the transition but was going to report to a new VP of Marketing & Communications.

Eventually, the company hired an extremely bright 39-year-old female offering her a compensation package of $230k.

What sealed the deal was her extensive background in multiple facets of integrated marketing with a progressive Fortune 500 company.

Do you think Andrew's age was a liability?

In a recent AARP survey, only three percent of older employees have ever made a formal complaint of age discrimination to someone in the workplace.*

Are they simply accepting the job rejections? Shrugging off the denials for promotion? Or taking a buyout or early retirement?

My guess is…all the above.

Now, in Mary's circumstance, unless her company is ready to lawyer up or they are completely out of touch with reality, she is probably going to continue being a major player.

Here age is not going to be a factor, because she has demonstrated that she is advanced in technology, is highly sharp mentally and physically, and trying to replace her for someone younger who will work for less would be extremely counter-productive with a significant risk of revenue loss for the company.

And that would be just plain stupid, don't you think?

For Andrew, his age is going to be a liability.

Not because he has type 1 diabetes, is overweight, with a noticeable receding hairline.

His age is going to be a potential liability because the executive-level marketing/communication director roles he is applying for are asking for proficiencies with integrated marketing strategies and the ability to lead influential digital content management, along with a multinational team.

The requirements clearly outline several skills that Andrew has not bothered to embrace and although he states a willingness to develop professionally…

That ship has sailed.

For those who struggle with ageism, if you're gunning for a promotion or heading into a job interview, you may want to touch up the gray, dress a bit youthful, and act like technology is your best friend.

Many of us concur that age is a state of mind and I'm not suggesting you run out and get Botox and start shopping at H&M.

However, do you think going into an interview looking like you made a quantum leap from 1991 and making statements like "I never go on LinkedIn" are initially positioning you for success either?

If you're 50+ and looking to exclusively be a 'farmer' with no interest in being a 'hunter' (or a happy medium).

Or, trying to convince a hiring decision-maker that your maturity and devotion to one company should be a considerable factor in positioning you over a younger candidate.

It might be time to consider a new role...
Like checking membership cards at Costco!

Remember predator vs prey? The older, slower antelope most likely will be consumed by a younger, hungrier predator.

In today's job market, many silver foxes that still have some skin in the game before retirement may need to aggressively embrace and familiarize themselves with new technology and workflow processes.

If they choose not to...then yes...
I guess that can be attributed to age after all.

Chapter Nine

Work Gaps and Job Hoppers

In April 2020, the universe was drastically altered, and life as we knew it was about to change!

Thanks to COVID-19, employee furloughs were ushered in before they turned into permanent layoffs.

And for many Americans, that was okay.

Between stimulus packages and a generous unemployment spiff, these individuals now had some time to reflect on their careers and what their next move was going to be.

Categorically speaking, many quickly returned to the workforce.

Others rode it out as long as they could before putting the keys in the ignition and driving back to reality.

Then there are some still holding out for the ideal work-from-home remote job.

Now, you don't need a global pandemic to create a work gap.

Health issues, bad luck in finding employment, parenting, or taking care of a loved one can facilitate that as well.

Regardless of the situation, too many work gaps on a resumé can jam up a potential candidate like eating too much cheese!

However, some medicine offering fast, effective relief will not be so effective in explaining why they have not been working.

Believe it or not, work gaps are going to be more commonplace in the future, but that doesn't mean you're not being productive

From an employment standpoint, as one month turns into six months....then a year, frustration can manifest into full-blown depression.

For many, it's not about getting a job (there are plenty out there), it's about finding that one job that was relatable in function and compensation.

If you had extended periods of unemployment regardless of the reason, stating that on your resumé is strictly taboo!

A hiring manager doesn't want to read that your plant closed, or your company merged with a global conglomerate, or you became a stay-at-home parent.

There is simply no need to draw a hiring decision-maker a map outlining why you were not gainfully employed during an extended period.

Maria was a purchasing manager for Exxon from February of 2012 until she was permanently laid off in July of 2018 due to the plant's closing.

She reached out to me a few months later to help with her resumé, and after several interviews, she finally landed a new job with a company called HME in March of 2019 where she was still presently employed.

Although she was thankful for going back to work, after a year, she told me that unfortunately, the job was failing to meet her expectations, so she contacted me again to update her resumé putting her current role on it.

However, she was very concerned about her eight-month work gap and how it was going to make her look.

After listening empathically, I assured her that permanent lay-offs were common in the workforce and she did nothing wrong during her period of unemployment.

I further explained that it takes time to find something comparable, and many HR managers are not going to be hung up on an eight-month work gap.

Although I put her mind at ease…slightly, I knew it wasn't going to be enough.

So, I simply took the months off the work history!

HME, Corp, Savannah, MO | **2019 to Present**
(Instead of 03/2019 to Present)

Exxon, Barrow MO | **2012 to 2018**
(Instead of 02/2012 to 07/2018)

Now, Maria doesn't have an eight-month work gap jumping off her resumé!

Another option to consider is adding volunteering, independent consulting, or freelance work.

Listing a 'side hustle' is still better than leaving a work gap. Just make sure your section is not titled PROFESSIONAL EXPERIENCE.

Consider changing it to WORK HISTORY or WORK EXPERIENCE.

It's not very sexy, but it's still better than nothing!

Martin was a highly talented, mid-level quality engineering manager at an automobile manufacturing plant.

For the past 15 years, he moved up with the company starting as a college intern progressing rapidly to higher levels of responsibility.

Once the company decided to consolidate its large SUV division, he was left with two options:

1. Take a lower-level position across the country uprooting his family and leaving other loved ones behind.

2. Accept the severance package and move on down the road.

Well, Martin took the severance hoping that he was going to find something similar within his market. However, there was one hiccup...

His market didn't have a ton of industrial options let alone another large auto manufacturing facility in the area.

For the first couple of months, thanks to his severance, he took care of items around the house, became more active in his kids' extracurricular functions, and didn't put a lot of emphasis on finding a new role, let alone get his resumé in order.

Besides, he also had a wide network of friends and peers that he could probably reach out to for new opportunities.

After a few weeks, Martin decided it was time to start putting a plan into action. At this point, you might be wondering:

"Why is Martin only now putting an action plan together?"

"Didn't he know his job with the company was in jeopardy?"

Yes and no.

You would think that with sales being drastically reduced in the large SUV market, combined with the demand for mid-size, hybrid, and electric SUVs, that sooner or later, Martin's company was going to have to shift gears (no pun intended).

Perhaps he was hoping that his department was going to start mass-producing a different line of SUVs?

At this stage, the smart play would have been to see the writing on the wall and recognize that despite his superior saying his job was safe for now (and it may have well been), there was a chance that over the next several months, his position could be in jeopardy.

In my experience, the probability that a superior is going to be completely transparent about the future of their department is probably 50/50…and that is a kind estimate.

So, Martin began putting his resumé together with the help of his wife and a few friends. Then, he uploaded it on Indeed and began trolling around on LinkedIn.

He didn't bother to modify it, instead, he just sent the same one for every single job (Spray and Pray).

After a while, he was beginning to get perturbed that manufacturing companies were not breaking down his door for an interview.

Sure, he was getting contacted by recruiters for selling funeral plots, life insurance, and automobile sales, but that simply wasn't in Martin's plan.

As the weeks turned into months, Martin was not so engaging anymore.

And his wife was becoming even more frustrated.

This wasn't because of his lack of employment…it was his lack of communication (and intimacy).

Furthermore, his enthusiasm was replaced with a short wick of a temper. He was like a time bomb ready to go off at any second!

And Martin's career mojo was in a complete tailspin!

Geraldo was a safety officer for a major food manufacturing plant. He was also a valued and dedicated employee starting on the assembly line, then progressed into a supervisory position before finally being promoted to his most recent management role.

One day, his company announced a merger with a global food conglomerate and word around the watercooler was that they were considering consolidating operations with their Juarez, Mexico facility.

Now, Geraldo had sensed that there was a chance his plant might be closing eventually, so he decided to take a proactive approach.

He reached out to me to put his resumé together and get his career options in order since he already determined that's he wasn't going to relocate for a substantial pay loss.

Six months later (right on cue) the new company announced that unfortunately, it was closing Geraldo's plant at the end of the year.

As part of the management team, Geraldo was going to stay on board during this transition until the lights were turned off for good (like going down with the ship).

Unlike Martin, Geraldo began putting out his resumé immediately, but over the next several months, he was also struggling with getting hired for other facility management roles.

I modified his resumé accordingly and he didn't have a problem getting interviews. He even made it to the final round on several occasions before the position was offered to someone else.

Was Geraldo discouraged?

Hell yeah, he was (who wouldn't be?).

Throughout his unemployment, Geraldo decided to step up and become one of the event organizers for the annual Hispanic Heritage Festival.

This involved working with community leaders, city officials, volunteers, and vendors and allowed him to utilize his organization, time management, and other leadership skills while helping a great cause.

It wasn't facilities management, and he wasn't getting paid, but he was still handling plenty of responsibilities.

Ironically, he discovered that his leadership skills had improved, rather than regressed!

When he was a facility safety manager, he was always toying with getting his Project Management Professional (PMP) certification.

Now, since he had some free time, he decided to move forward and complete this certification (which is very weighted in his field).

Once the festival was over, I updated his resumé accordingly.

Now, instead of having a work gap, he was able to highlight his recent accomplishments and include his PMP certification (which could have factored in not being selected for those other positions).

By changing his PROFESSIONAL EXPERIENCE section to WORK HISTORY, he was able to capitalize on his role as an event organizer and we structured it accordingly:

Hispanic Heritage Festival | 2019
Volunteer Event Organizer
-   Accountable for a volunteer team of approximately 20 individuals. Negotiated with vendors on food and safety products and coordinated with city zoning officials on obtaining all the necessary permits to prevent any potential issues during the event setup.
-   Played an instrumental role in setting a new attendance record with over 8,000 attendees that generated approximately $18,000 for local charities.

It wasn't long after the festival ended that Geraldo finally nailed a new gig as a facilities manager.

Between that and his community leadership recognition…

His career mojo was back in full swing!

On the flipside of a work gap, is having to explain why there are too many different jobs on a resumé.

This can easily be interpreted as a job hopper or workplace cancer.

But this is not always the case.

For example, how can you define someone who has worked for eight employers spanning 10 years?
-   Contracted roles
-   Traveling Nurse
-   Mergers & Acquisitions
-   Always recruited by other companies

Raj has worked in several IT capacities as a contractor for 14 years.

Over this period, he has supported several multi-cloud integrations and solution architecture projects lasting anywhere from six months to two years.

However, he doesn't mention on his resumé that he was a contractor and lists each project as an employer for each company (This is a common misrepresentation, that many times is not intentional).

In this situation, he worked for only two contractors.

Once I restructured his work history it made more sense:

Cognizant | **2015** to **Present**

Led several projects for a global technology solutions provider delivering digital go-to-market (GTM) strategy and integrated solutions for six different companies valued at over $24 million.

These included the following:

- Implemented a digital corporate strategy for a Fortune 100 insurance company streamlining private mobile networking, Edge computing, IoT, and next-generation application development.

- Played a pivotal role in launching out an initial go-to-market engagement strategy for a high-tech cloud enterprise that involved the complex designing of the company's computing strategy, adoption plans, and application infrastructure.

TEK Systems | **2007** to **2015**

Collaborated with IT leadership teams for several Fortune 500 companies on integrated marketing campaigns, content management, and pre-sales engagement. Presented clear and concise action plans to executives to outline potential return on investments (ROI).

- Empowered a team of three engineers to create a data platform for a growing pharmaceutical company utilizing Apache Kafka resulting in a 25% reduction in core application data ingestion time to service computational research.

- Implemented a go-to-market framework for a leading data solutions provider. This project deliverable spanned two years valued at $5 million.

By consolidating his contracting roles, it painted a clearer picture of his dedication to only two companies instead of trying to explain eight of them.

Of course, there is always that one individual who either has issues working with others, is very shady, or perhaps...a good bull-shitter who seems to find a way to land a new gig with regularity.

Now, I have two general policies:
1. Never judge or make assumptions about a client's character.
2. Refrain from fabrication or outright misrepresentation.

But there is nothing wrong with a little vagueness.
And that takes some creativity.

Sometimes, it is not necessary to list every role (especially if the job lasted less than six months). Therefore, I may recommend not even listing it, or determine which of the roles has the most relevancy.

By removing less relevant jobs, it should be easier to 'camouflage' the work history.

That is about as close as I get to 'bending the law' without breaking, it, so to speak.

Some professionals are fortunate to be consistently coveted by other companies, and depending on the market, bouncing around every couple of years, may not pose any red flags.

But what percentage are we talking about?

It will be interesting to see how job markets will be impacted by extremely aggressive recruiting on any level.

Regardless of the situation, I foresee a pattern where loyalty and dedication to one employer will continue to diminish.

And both the employee and employer are accountable for this, unfortunately.

Chapter 10

Should I Vax or Should I Go?

It is with increased frequency that I find potential clients reaching out to me to say they are quitting their jobs without any contingency plan or vision on where they want to go, and what they are searching for.

Chalk it up to COVID mandates, bad work culture, being asked to do more with less, or just being tired of all the bullshit that goes into the daily grind of being accountable to perform at a certain level.

I get it.

For almost 20 years, my typical cycle consisted of the dreaded Monday turning into 'Hump Day' Wednesday, then Friday, usually working half-day on Saturday, and by Sunday afternoon I was already dreading Monday again.

Not the kind of work/life balance you want to have.

As I was putting this book together, a dear friend of mine sent me a book that was penned by The Dalai Lama.

For those who are not familiar with the teachings of his Holiness (including myself), there were several references in his book on how we define true happiness.

Keep in mind, I am not advocating that we convert to Tibetan Buddhism or any religion for that matter.

The common thread I discovered was how, as a society, we refine our goals when it comes to self-pleasure.

Whether it is money, status, security, recognition, or all the above...

How much stock do we REALLY put into health and happiness?

For someone who migrates into the U.S. from an impoverished third-world country, receives an H1 sponsorship, before earning a Green card, that individual might have to work back-breaking hours doing three jobs to make $40,000 to feed his family of five.

But, that person might be making a fraction of that in his home country while dodging drug cartels.

Do you think he is extremely grateful to have this opportunity?

To analyze this in more depth, say you were brought up in a middle-class environment instead of a poverty-stricken third-world setting...

Ask yourself, how happy would you be in this situation?

My guess would be... not very much.

What is also a sad situation, are those who deem themselves a failure if they are not making six figures especially when they see their friends and acquaintances in that income range.

Now, you might be thinking, geez Kevin, how can you compare the two?

My answer is an easy one.

If you had to experience making ends meet in a country filled with internal strife, civil war, authoritarian rule, and an inflation rate that makes currency almost worthless…

Your vision of wealth might be a little more alternated.

Sound extreme?

Does the U.S. have its share of problems…of course, but in our society, many of us simply do not equate our issues at home versus abroad, except when we watch any international news from the comfort of our homes equipped with running water and electricity.

Bob was a senior-level pharmaceutical account manager who moved through the ranks with several major pharma companies spanning 20 years.

As a highly targeted, svelte collegiate athlete, who gave good face, he was coveted by several medical device and drug companies for his ability to thrive in high-pressure situations with a commitment to continuously improving in a team environment.

Throughout his career, he was a constant quota-buster, regularly walking across that stage every year earning award recognition trips to exotic destinations throughout the globe.

His star was always rising and it was not surprising that recruiters were aggressively seeking out his services as he moved into marketing advanced Immuno-oncology drugs.

By this time, Bob's total annual compensation package (salary, commission, and bonuses) was around $450,000.

With this kind of jack, his spouse and kids were well-taken care of.

They lived in a beautiful sprawling home, went to the best schools, drove high-end vehicles, went on adventurous trips while enjoying the comfort and security that comes with making this kind of bank.

But there was another cost associated with this lifestyle...

Bob was burned out.

Between the kazillion frequent flyer miles he earned from flying all over the country, the 60-hour work-weeks, and the constant demands to make his nut each quarter, the pressure to continuously perform at an All-Star level was beginning to weigh on Bob.

Spending most of his time on the road, Bob is eating out all the time. In addition, he is wooing physicians, drug manufacturers, staff members, and other major decision-makers by taking them to sporting events and golf outings.

Not a bad gig, eh?

But it has taken its toll.

Although Bob was only in his late 40's, he was already showing significant signs of aging. His hair was almost gray, he had put on 50 pounds, and he was developing symptoms of a stomach ulcer.

One day, as he was driving to an appointment, he was having trouble catching his breath. This had happened sporadically over the past several weeks but he rationalized that it was just a little stress combined with allergies.

But this time his heart rate was rapidly accelerating!

At the wife's urgency, he went in for a stress test on his heart which fortunately was a good thing, since they discovered he had a partial blockage in one of his arteries and had to have a stint put in.

His triglyceride level was well above the norm for a man of his age which also contributed to his condition.

Interestingly enough, he didn't have a family history of heart-related issues.

When we spoke, Bob had confessed to me that the money he was making was simply not worth the quality of life he was living, and being away for extended periods from his family.

He stressed that there was no point in trying to make as much as possible if it meant a non-existent work-life balance?

Worse, where he might be in 10 years?

Initially, I told him how **_unfortunate_** his situation was (but not the money) however, Bob quickly shifted gears and said he was **_extremely fortunate_**!

Not because of what he accumulated over the years, but the warning signs he took to heart (no pun intended).

He added that trying to maintain his current pace simply wasn't worth taking a chance on not being around to see his grandkids or spending his golden years enjoying what he had amassed.

There is something else to consider when we think about success.

Our fear of failure.

What I am about to confess, was for years, something I was ashamed of.

Worse, for most of my life, I had no idea how to cope with it.

I call it... The 'Big Three.'
1. ADHD
2. Depression
3. Social Anxiety.

During my 15 years of seamlessly networking with business leaders at public events, walking red carpets, and presenting programs to key decision-makers...

I was putting on an act so to speak.

Because of my social anxiety, I always knocked back some vodka before I went to events to filter out the awkwardness I was constantly feeling.

I would sit in the car building up some form of confidence before pitching to a client large or small.

My ability to be organized and focused on the tasks at hand was all over the place.

Looking back on all of this, I'm surprised my career didn't spiral out of control.

Although I thought I was success-driven...

I was transfixed on worrying about failure.

My ups and downs could be attributed to several factors primarily centered on my work performance.

However, even hobbies like golf... or someone's opinion of me played a role as well.

For some reason, these would typically revolve around quarters throughout the year.

Examples of having a good quarter:
- Hitting my sales numbers.
- Landing a big account.
- Receiving phrase from a client.
- Hitting my drives down the fairway with some consistency.

During these periods, I was filled with excitement and optimism!

Examples of having a bad quarter:

- Losing a large account without finding a new one to replace it with.
- Low commissions.
- Issues with clients and family.
- Slicing and hooking my drives consistently off the tee.

During these periods of darkness... my life was shit.

Getting out of bed in the morning was a challenge.

I felt embarrassed about my performances which would isolate me from friends, family, and co-workers.

And worse...this was leading to suicidal thoughts.

I know...stupid right?

Although they were lingering, and I could never go through with it, I was ashamed and guilty for even considering this option because of how it would impact others.

This is also the first time I have ever revealed this publicly.

In hindsight, I never had it that bad.

My professional career for the most part has been filled with achievements and awards, I lived comfortably and I was surrounded by family and friends who cared deeply for me.

But it was the small bits of negatives that engulfed all the positives.

Why?

Because it is a mental condition.

And like many conditions, they simply do not go away magically.

The only thing you can do is manage it.

Fortunately, I have my wife Stacey to thank for pushing me to seek help once and for all with dealing with "The Big Three.'

And it was a game-changer!

It might have been a stretch to try and be this successful without seeking help… and it has nothing to do with money or accolades.

When I packed my box in January of 2018, my success had become rooted in helping others with their careers.

One day, maybe I'll have millions of dollars, but do I give a shit?

Nope!

Of course, I want to be comfortable financially...

But I'll take good health and sanity any day.

Many individuals do not live out their dreams. Sure, they have a plan, but many times it does not come to fruition.

In some instances, their circumstances prevent them from saying screw it…I'm outta here!

So, was I lucky?

No doubt!

But I also created some of my own luck, and this goes back to finding something I was truly gifted in and running with it.

Also, I had laid down some groundwork before my flight into full-time business ownership like building a local following, capitalizing on my reputation as a feature writer for advertorials, my knowledge of how to optimize a business and individuals digitally, and getting my branding and website in order.

To say that I burned the candle at both ends is a gross understatement!

Between my everyday job and All-Write Local Resumés, my

typical workday started around 6 am and ended around 10 pm almost seven days a week for over a year.

It finally came to a head...

80-hour work-weeks sucked!

Something had to give.

Should I stay the course as a multimedia account executive, or do my own thing.

You can guess which path I eventually took.

Now, I am not advocating that everyone just pack their shit and do their own thing.

In my case, I was methodical and had this well planned out in advance.

Remember the old saying...

'Those that fail to plan...plan to fail.'

Realistically, I am also very cognizant that everything I have worked for can be taken from me in an instant.

Many times, I work with clients who have been business owners and for whatever reason, they decide to venture back into the job market.

Some are fine with tossing the headaches that come with being completely accountable into the garbage. Also, going back to collecting a regular paycheck, having decent health insurance, and having a company match a percentage of their 401K.

Others are more deflated because of all the work they had put in. However, because of circumstances beyond their control, (family matters, the business environment, lack of demand, etc...) they are forced to close the doors.

And then there are those who didn't put that much effort into it or realized that it was a lot more work than they anticipated.

Regardless of the situation, there is still some deflation… it just depends on the level.

What you take away from that experience is what strengthens your career swag.

Usually, January is by far, my busiest month since one of the top New Years' resolutions besides weight loss and quitting smoking….is searching for a new job.

"This year is going to be the year of change!"

"Take this job and shove it!"

"My time and talents are underappreciated!"

Over time, I have noticed a radical shift in the way people are quitting their jobs.

No notice…

No letter of resignation…

They are simply walking out!

Thank you, COVID-19.

Why do I blame the wretched virus you ask?

As I reflect on an 18-month period where many people were working from home, watching those suffer through the loss of someone close (including myself), and witnessing individuals revert back to a people-facing grind, it would be naive to think that this had not taken a tremendous toll on many people in the workforce on all levels.

People have to go back to dressing a certain way, grooming, commuting to work, finding childcare, and worrying about taking time off work for quarantining (themselves or their kids and loved ones).

Since many employers have been doing more with less, work-life balance has shifted back to a work-work routine.

Businesses are having to pick up the slack due to a shortage of able-bodied individuals who are electing to stay home.

Like many industries, supply chain and logistics have been hit especially hard during this period.

We have the goods but they have been sitting in ports due to the lack of resources to get them from Point A to Point B.

The transportation industry has been wrestling with driver shortages for years, and it's going to get a whole lot worse if we do not find a way to put more butts in those seats.

Perhaps the U.S. should issue more H1 visas to those willing to work?

How about a substantial increase in pay stemming from a generous performance-based incentive?

One thing is for sure...a $15-an-hour minimum wage is simply not going to cut it!

Or even $20 an hour

Think about this...

Let's take someone with a spouse and two kids who works a 40-hour week with five hours of overtime.

- 40x20=$800 + 30x5=150 for a total of $950 a week.
- Now, take out 20% for taxes/social security (-$190).
- Health Insurance (-$125)
- Let's not forget the 401K (5% -$45)

Now, they would be taking home $590 a week or approximately $2,300 to $2,900 per month (depending on a four or five-week month).

Now, let's say their rent/home loan is $1,000 per month.
Their car loan is $249 per month.
Utilities $250 per month (12-month average)
This leaves roughly around $1,000 per month for disposable income used for food, activities, vacation, school supplies, clothing.
And I didn't even include any daycare expenses, credit card payments, or putting any money aside for college.
This is why the two-income household is a necessity for most average Americans.
We know the credit card companies are having a field day!

So, let's say one spouse walks away from their job. They are not going to receive unemployment, so I'm scratching my head and wondering: "how a family of four these days can survive comfortably taking home one income consisting of $25,000?"
I'll tell you.
Massive credit card debt, missed payments, and some extreme belt-tightening!
But this is happening more frequently as well.

On the opposite end of this spectrum is a statistic taken from the US Census Bureau which states that the percentage of Americans who make a salary over $100K is around five percent!
So for the other 95%...don't bang your head against the wall.
You are well above the majority!

Thanks to social media sites like Facebook and Tik Tok there is a new resource spreading conflicting views on the long-term effects of getting vaccinated.

As a result, people are walking dogs, selling clothes online, or starting side gigs willing to work for less instead of being forced to get a vaccine shot.

Since this has significant impacts on career direction, I felt it appropriate to address these issues in a little more detail.

With COVID mandates rapidly being implemented, large companies, government employers, healthcare, and other industries are taking full advantage of weaving through HIPAA compliances.

Many have complained to me about how the government and private businesses can even communicate to their employees that unless they have been vaccinated against COVID-19 they will be terminated.

And my answer is a diplomatic one.

Do you think an HR department wants to invest any time in designing an exit strategy to address this ultimatum? Or getting a legal team involved?

This impacts productivity, bottom line, and profit margins just like a plant shutdown.

Several HR managers have told me that this is nothing more than a giant pain in the ass!

And they have better things to do than waste time implementing these policies.

Furthermore, who could blame them for feeling this way?

Legally, here is how employers can implement these mandates.

In short, if you work for a private company with no union contract, they can require employees to be vaccinated as a condition of employment as long as they allow exemptions for medical reasons and seriously held religious beliefs.

As long as a doctor or clergy will sign off on that.

Effective September 2021, President Biden had also reached deep into the playbook to get more Americans vaccinated by incorporating an emergency provision outlined in The Occupational Safety and Health Act (OSHA).

By using this compliance and his executive privilege as Chief Executive of the Federal Work Force he can withhold federal funding from hospitals, health care agencies, and other industries.

Also, as Commander in Chief of the Armed Forces, he can enforce this policy on all branches of the military as well.

How's that for a cherry on top!

For the record, these mandates have been around since 1905 when the Supreme Court ruled that the town of Cambridge, Massachusetts, could require all adults to be vaccinated against smallpox.*

So, by relying on the government's constitutional power to regulate commerce and OSHA's authority to issue emergency standards, the president CAN require companies to maintain safe workplaces through vaccination.

Isn't it ironic that when the pandemic first hit, individuals were waiting in lines all day just to get tested!

And many people ***would have paid a million dollars*** to get vaccinated if it was available then.

Fast forward one year later and we were witnessing many states ***offering people a million dollars*** in the form of lotteries attempting to get more people vaccinated!

What the hell is wrong with our society?

Why should we have to bribe someone to get a vaccine that could potentially save a person's life… or those around them?

Recently, I was speaking to a lady and her husband, and the subject of vaccinations came up.

She told me that because of her underlying health issues, she could not receive the vaccine.

Besides that, even if she could get it, she said she would exercise her right to refuse it because she didn't trust the FDA.

According to what she was reading on social media, it was a hoax to put more money in the pockets of pharmaceutical companies.

I listened very attentively and agreed that as Americans we should have the right to choose.

Throughout the afternoon, I noticed that she was consistently going outside to smoke a menthol cigarette.

When I bumped into her, I casually asked her what she thought was going to do more long-term harm to her…

The COVID shot…or those smokie treats?

I was met with a stupefied look, a head cocked to one side, and nothing close to a meaningful rebuttal.

Now, what does this have to do with career mojo?

Not much.

What does this have to do with being forced to get a vaccination to continue being gainfully employed?

More than you think.

If you state that your principles on being forced to get a COVID vaccine will be the tipping point for packing up your box, I strongly suggest rethinking that if it means walking away from a lucrative career.

What's worse, is using the constitution that millions of service members have fought for… as a shield!

I don't think our forefathers had that in mind when they wrote the Articles of Confederation back in 1777 (or when it was replaced by the US Constitution in 1789).

For those thinking of simply walking away, at least stop… and ask yourself why?

And what do you plan to do moving forward?

Seems simple right?

Last I checked, there were not a lot of remote jobs starting at $100K unless you are a senior-level, cutting-edge tech engineer.

Now if someone qualifies for retirement, that would be feasible, but what percentage are we talking about?

I take great pride in being able to help people transition into new industries by taking their plethora of experiences, digging deep into their toolbox, and optimizing their vast resources accordingly.

What I can not do, is help someone who has no clue as to who they are or try defining them as something they are not.

In other words, I cannot fabricate a job or conjure up a character who is a fast learner of whatever comes their way.

There must be some kind of framework, foundation, plan, or agenda.

Something!

In our society, we tend to be reactionary. In turn, we make hasty decisions.

This is why I have a standing policy...

If you are seeking resumé and career help because of one bad day, give it a couple of weeks.

Now, if you are still feeling the same way, then we can proceed further.

Sometimes, the situation requires more confidence-boosting, in this case, I would elect to refer them to a couple of life & wellness coaches.

After all, I'm not a therapist.

Another item to consider is all those individuals waiting in the wings who want an opportunity with that one company or role.

One person's trash could be another person's treasure.

Something to chew on if you decide to jettison your job.

According to SHRM, (Society of Human Resources Management), one of the best strategies to keep workers from fleeing is to offer incentives to them in the form of payments* (aka: bribe).

If all it was going to take was $250 to compromise one's principles and get the vaccine, then they probably need to find a new source for their fake news.

Even if you were receiving and submitting weekly COVID tests results was an alternative...who are we crapping?

It would be a pain in the ass!

But not everyone thinks like me.

So, why am I harping on this?

Because I feel this will be standard protocol in the workforce for years to come (long after this book has been published).

So... screw you COVID and all your future variants!

Chapter 11

Facts, Misconceptions, and the Future

Image making it to the final round of the interview. You show up, wait around, before being ushered into a conference room.

Your leg is bobbing up and down as you are nervously waiting for several key decision-makers from the department to walk in for a final round of questions.

But instead, the HR assistant walks in smiling.

As she coolly hands you bottled water, she also places an augmented reality (AR) simulator on the table and kindly asks you to put it on.

Yep...

Giant goggles!

But instead of playing a game, you are instructed to solve problems by touching and transferring objects so a third-party talent acquisition vendor can determine and assess your skills before the company makes its final decision.

I am not bull-shitting you when I say some companies have already migrated to this form of weeding out a candidate!

Now, if you have gotten this far in the book, then I saved the best for last, so before we progress into the 'New Way to Resumé' let's review some facts and misconceptions regarding the present and future ways to self-promote oneself.

Fact:

Many professionals aggressively looking for work, will have a much better chance of having recruiters reach out to them by having a **well-crafted LinkedIn profile.**

Why?

Because over 95% of recruiters are using this platform trolling for candidates globally.*

Many of my clients who are turned off by Facebook or Twitter seem to lump LinkedIn in this category…

Big mistake!

Now, just because I have been contracted by LinkedIn as one of their Resumé & Career Experts, I receive nothing for plugging their product. (But it would be nice!).

Personally, I just feel their platform is going to position a job candidate more effectively.

And here's my reason:

Establishes a candidate's credibility for potential new opportunities:

Think about it? Every time a recruiter reaches out to an individual, you can bet your ass they have looked at their profile.

A properly filled out and utilized LinkedIn profile page can instantly accomplish things that a resumé or CV cannot.

And that is positioning someone as an expert in their field(s) through postings, engagements, videos, articles, and photos.

Excellent opportunities to network with other professionals in your field.

Having connections in any form is still a key driver if you are searching for a new job or career.

Consider this as a digital Rolodex, which can be accessed at your disposal.

Furthermore, your connections could potentially introduce you to key decision-makers from various companies you are looking to work for.

Think of it as online namedropping.

And the best part... all of this is free! (For now).

Another suggestion if you are actively looking for new opportunities is to take advantage of their Premium member offer.

The first month is free, you can cancel at any time, and it gives you special features like in-mail access to the job poster, competitive intelligence on how you rank with other candidates, and skills you should have on your profile.

Fact:

A study done by The PEW Research Center revealed that **94% of job seekers use smartphones to explore new job opportunities.***

Job sites are now offering features that include sending your resumé with one click off your mobile device.

This is another reason I encourage using Word Doc. It is a simple, universal format that will allow for easier readability on a mobile device and penetrates any ATS.

This can also be converted off Google Docs, and a receiver doesn't have to 'pitch and stretch' like they would for a PDF file.

Fact:

Videos and virtual resumés will help build your personal brand.

There is nothing wrong with adding a video link URL to your resumé or as I mentioned, your LinkedIn profile.

This can demonstrate innovation, creativity, and showcases to potential employers your virtual engagement strengths that cannot be conveyed on a traditional resumé.

However, I am not advocating replacing your traditional resumé completely with a virtual one.

Misconception:

"I'm going to always be bypassed for certain jobs because I lack a degree"

In case you haven't noticed this on job postings these days, but many companies are electing to list similar work experience in place of a degree.

Do you want to know why?

Because they are losing out on qualified candidates who have accumulated the certifications, training, and real-time work experience that cannot be taught in the classroom!

If I had to list the number one factor that my clients over the age of 30 struggle with...

It's not earning a Bachelors' Degree.

Furthermore, it is one of the foundations for losing that career mojo!

But it doesn't have to be that way.

Many of my clients who are employed or fulfilling the hardest job in the world (the stay-at-home parent) have considered earning online degrees.

And over the years, many of them ask me if they are worth getting?

Yes and No.

Certainly, colleges and universities will have conflicting thoughts on this, but how far will a Bachelors' Degree in Sociology or History take someone these days?

Unless your immediate strategy includes an advanced degree, you better start looking at your career options as a labor of love, because you may find it challenging to make tons of money from it. (And that's okay too if you are not that materialistic).

These days many Bachelors' degrees seem to be a prerequisite for earning an advanced degree.

Of course, there are those technical roles that require undergrad degrees like engineering, biotechnology, and advanced medical...

But what percentage of the student population fall in that category?

Now, you might think that I am contradicting myself since I mentioned in earlier chapters about the personal investment in going back and finishing your education or completing an advanced degree to stay competitive in the job market.

However, there are plenty of certifications to set yourself apart from other candidates, for example:

- Lean Six Sigma
- PMP (Project Manager Professional)
- SHRM (Society for Human Resources Management)
- SAFe® (Scaled Agile Framework)
- Scrum Master

Now, there are plenty of intangible benefits besides the course curriculums that the college experience provides...

Like teamwork.

Especially if you were a student-athlete who also had the task of juggling academics with athletics.

This is a special trait coveted by many sales organizations, particularly pharmaceutical and medical device companies.

But again, what percentage are we talking about?

Less than two percent?

It is very frustrating to see young college students who are getting ready to enter the workforce list their only relevant experience over their last four years as serving as the Chairperson of the Spring Fling and working at a local bar & grill.

If you cannot snag a decent internship in your related field of study...

How are you going to pivot into a decent entry-level role?

You better hope you come into some serious shoulder-tapping!

It is also unfortunate that the trend over the last 20 years includes blue-collar roles and the trades taking a backseat to higher education.

Who do you think utilizes more problem solving and critical thinking skills?

Someone with a degree in general studies or an electrician?

Also, who is likely going to have a decent starting salary, a pension, and no student loan to pay off?

Traditionally, many teens have been brain-washed into thinking that any college degree leads to higher-paying jobs with plenty of security.

God forbid if they decide to go into construction, plumbing, or pipefitting!

Misconception:

You need to submit a cover letter for every job you apply for.

I may also get some static for this one, but according to Zety.com, in 2021, only 26% of recruiters who even read cover letters stated that it influenced them to move forward with a candidate.*

Now, it's a no-brainer to attach a cover letter if the job gives you the option, or they specifically ask for one.

But what if the job posting does not make any reference to attaching a cover letter?

In many circles, job seekers are told to play it safe and send one anyway.

But here is where this can land in the bullshit patch.

What if your cover letter sucks?

If I had to pool the percentage of HR managers, I have consulted with that are not that interested in a cover letter, I would put it at 50/50.

However, if an employer wants a cover letter that bad...or tries to 'test' an applicant to see how committed they are to that job, at least they should include that option somewhere on the job posting.

Also, if the so-called 'experts' are telling you that a general cover is better than no cover letter at all...

How does that convey that you are a good fit for that role?

You cannot half-ass a cover letter, many hiring managers will smell that funk a mile awhile.

Like the resumé itself, it should demonstrate your skills and abilities and some specific examples of how you are going to make an impact for that company's promoted position.

Now, I am not advocating that you write every cover letter from scratch...but at least have the flexibility to tailor it accordingly.

Here is an example of a cover letter that is tailored for an Office Manager position. Specifically, this company is looking for someone who also has experience supporting finance functions, software, and technical implementations and can thrive in a hybrid setting (office and remote).

I left off any personal info, day and year, and a closing (but you should include them).

To whom it may concern,

Recently, I discovered that Yorkee Solutions was seeking a versatile, enthusiastic office manager to deliver administrative and technical support services on-site and remotely.

Over the last 10 years, I have performed multiple roles, including office administration, HR, technology implementation, and finance management. During this time, I have collaborated with cross-functional teams driving continuous improvements in workforce solutions, payroll, and billing.

In addition, I have cultivated robust relationships with suppliers, vendors, and other business partners.

Strategically speaking, I utilize analytical problem solving and creative decision-making to efficiently filter and prioritize daily activities which have served me well in overcoming obstacles and promptly addressing issues before they escalate.

After carefully reviewing the requirements and qualifications for this position, some examples of my experiences and projects that can contribute significantly to this role include the following:

- During my time at XYX, I transitioned my department to a remote environment utilizing Zoom and GoToMeeting with minimal disruptions in workflow.

- As an office manager, I successfully integrated legacy payroll systems to ADP, PAYCHEX, and PAYCOR and supported several IT conversions and database migrations.

In closing, if Yorkee is looking for an employee-centric, passionate office leader who is proficient in tech support and thrives in a hybrid setting, I am that person and look forward to discussing the value I can bring to this role.

Thank you again for considering me as a potential candidate.

In this mock-up, notice how I include relevant items that will position the candidate more favorably.

As I reflect to 2005 when I wrote my first resumé professionally, I paid special attention to slick-looking formats, quality paper (with the watermark in the upright position), complemented with a solid cover letter.

You could still email it to someone directly, didn't have to worry about having it screened by a robot and recruiters were not very technical when it came to weeding out a quality candidate.

Indeed was six months old (Nov 2004).

ZipRecruiter wasn't going to be launched for another five years.

LinkedIn was two years old (May 2003).

Fast forward to the present day.

The traditional format Baby Boomers and Gen Xers have been used to, have been taken over by Artificial Intelligence (AI), Machine Learning, and Augmented (AR), and Virtual Reality (VR).

Many of you may be scratching your head...

But this is what the future of job-seeking might look like.

These days, even high school students are completing LinkedIn profiles as part of their college application process.

Also, many progressive global companies are asking for a candidate to submit recorded speeches, videos, and other forms of multimedia in addition to their resumé.*

Even before COVID, more companies have elected to use platforms like HireVue to conduct initial interview screenings.

Moving forward, some experts also predict that AI and algorithms will play a larger role in determining a potential candidate based on their potential for success...before they are even interviewed!

In the future, you can expect companies to employ even more technological processes to analyze an applicant's characteristics that cannot be conveyed on a traditional resumé.

And those are... confidence and conviction!

In addition, some 'so-called experts' predict that future job seekers will need to think differently on how to write their resumé.

They are claiming that the AI process for selecting qualified applicants will not be based so much on their past experiences but on self-awareness, key strengths, passions, interests, and a vision for their careers.

Isn't that what the interview process is for?

If a candidate's previous work experience is a poor indicator of their potential.

Then why even go to work?

Call me old-school, but I still call this is a very lazy method of initially determining talent.

There was an article I was checking out: 'Employment Law, Red Flags in the Use of Artificial Intelligence in Hiring' by Gary D. Friedman and Thomas McCarthy.*

I liked how they pointed out that applicant tracking systems are only as good as the programmers who write the algorithm and 'feed the machine.' *

So, how competent are these programmers?

Many times, I must explain to my clients that it may not be their background or resumé, but a vendor or HRIS manager who did a piss-poor job in setting the applicant filters.

Every day, I am scanning through LinkedIn and read comments from disgruntled job seekers regarding the hiring process.

And they most certainly have valid reasons to gripe!

If it takes a company six or seven interviews to uncover that 'unicorn,' I hope the AI and Machine Learning strategy will play a role in whittling that number down.

Shouldn't that be beneficial for all parties?

With all this artificial bullshit determining whether an individual is the right job fit, the time was right to develop an integrated career strategy concept that drills down into all facets of the job-seeking process.

To me, it's ludicrous for anyone to seek out three separate services (resumé writing, interview coaching, and career consulting) that could lead to spending thousands of dollars.

This will only lead to contradiction…and confusion!

If anyone wants to dispute this, feel free to contradict.

When I started All-Write Local Resumés back in 2011, my focus was on writing resumés and cover letters. These were still printed out, put in an envelope, and even included a disc.

As LinkedIn became more popular, I was adding profiles and optimization to my repertoire.

Then in January 2018, I formed Resumedics Career Strategies & Solutions with an eye on a rapidly evolving digital hiring process.

When people ask me for an elevator pitch on what I do, I prefer to position it like a burrito.

By taking 'ingredients' like resumé writing, interview prep, a cover letter, a LinkedIn profile, and more importantly, a large helping of career development consulting, I wrap it up into a single entity that is fast, affordable… and leaves a client satisfied!

Sure, there are those mom & pop businesses, restaurants, retail, warehousing, and job fairs where someone will simply accept a printed resumé.

But you could go to Kinkos to have that done.

My objective for implementing a 'New Way to Resume' wasn't just to meet the needs of some niche market, but to provide an option to strengthen a client's chances in a digital hiring environment while architecting a career map for them.

In plain English, I teach them how to extract and interpret their backgrounds and skills to properly align them to new opportunities.

The key drivers include:
- Reviewing job postings to properly optimize a resumé.
- Walking the client through the resumé top-to-bottom explaining why it is structured in a certain manner, so they can speak effectively to it during an interview.
- Teaching them the methodologies behind what I am doing and its' relevance.
- Providing ongoing follow-up for future opportunities.

In other words, a partnership!

If you decide to write your resumé for a new career opportunity, may I suggest the following steps before you proceed:

1. See what's available in the marketplace before you crack open your laptop.
2. Establish a behavioral pattern centered on what these companies want and how you are going to favorable position your qualifications.
3. Analyze the pros & cons of a new career move. Examine items like retirement & health benefits and other 'hidden paychecks.'

Typically, I fancy myself as a realist...sprinkled with optimism.

For example, I believe that there are plenty of companies out there who will recognize the true value in someone and train that right person...regardless of their background or lack of experience.

Not because of compassion... but out of necessity.

Especially since many who were considering going back to work are saying "Screw this, I'm not wasting $3.50 a gallon in gas to drive my ass to an office where I can be micro-managed in person, while paying an additional $300 a week in daycare!"

Whether an employer initially evaluates a candidate by a robot, third-party vendor…or the old-fashion way with a firm handshake, it is still important to try and familiarize yourself with these three components:
1. The company's background
2. The influential decision-makers
3. The job itself.

Making these connections will set a foundation for developing the confidence and conviction needed to sell YOUR personal brand!

When I say personal brand, I emphasize to my clients to view their services no different than a professional athlete or entertainer.

Aren't they investing their time, skills, and experience to make an organization better in a competitive landscape?

Then they should be treated as a valuable commodity considering that without their services, where would the state of an employer be?

If I close my eyes and view my futuristic world, I envision highly talented, sought-after professionals on any level having their own agent representing them just like they do for pro athletes and entertainers.

They would meet with the key decision-makers, position their client as to why they would be a valuable piece to contributing to the mission and vision of that company, and even negotiate a favorable salary for their client based on market analysis.

This would eliminate the need for multiple tests, be more time-efficient for all parties involved, and give that candidate a fighting chance.

Recruiters could migrate into agents and still be paid a commission if their client gets hired.

In addition, receive an additional spiff if their client lasts at least a year with that company.

If we move into an employee-controlled job market, you never know what the future may hold.

Perhaps I should investigate that option.

Instead of being a career strategist, I can be...

A career agent!

Leo Burnett, one of the most iconic advertising executives of all time and named by Time Magazine as one of the 100 most influential people of the 20th century had a quirky, yet impactful quote:

"When you reach for the stars, you may not quite get them ...but you won't come up with a handful of mud either."

Losing that career mojo can be as crippling as any physical limitation, however, with some support from those we trust and value, we also have the power to persevere!

I have always lived by these four words:
'Nothing ventured... nothing gained."

And I hope many of you can embrace this as well!

Epilogue

Maybe it's just me.

But sometimes when I speak or consult with people regarding resumés and career strategy, I have this feeling that I am conveying information that people already know.

Kinda like playing the role of 'Captain Obvious.'

However, I find that this is not the case.

Of course, this is a seamless process for me, I have been doing it for ten years!

I assume that this is all common sense.

But I quickly suppress those thoughts.

The fact is, resumé writing done the right way (no pun intended) is hard for most individuals, these days more than ever.

It's more than just a well-written sentence and grammar-free content. These days, you have free software, like Grammarly, or built-in editors on laptops spellchecking for us.

There are millions of tutorials, templates, job boards, and other people's resumés that can be easily pilfered off the internet, therefore, generating one doesn't take much effort.

What one must stop and think about is...

How the resumé represents that individual outside of their work history, education, and skills.

Can you effectively sell it to a hiring-decision maker?

Can you effectively speak to it top-to-bottom?

If someone needs to have a resumé written merely as a formality to keep on file, this book is not going to provide much benefit.

This digs much deeper.

The stories you have read about have been recreated to protect the innocent…so to speak.

They are all actual experiences I have worked with that are brought to the surface to illustrate the diverse situations that individuals face every day as they wrestle with career change.

However, these are just a few of the hundreds of situations I have worked with over the years.

Although I only use first names, they are still altered because of confidentiality compliances. Therefore, if you feel any of these examples definitely 'out you', it is only coincidental.

You might be thinking that the tips and guidance I provided throughout this book are easier said than done,

And you would be spot on.

Just like the clients I have worked with, I simply focus on bringing a different perspective that resonates with people.

Fortunately, in many cases, it has positively altered the way they see themselves professionally without insulting anyone's intelligence.

Unfortunately, I am not a wizard, and can not magically transform everyone.

I strive to be impeccable, simply if that means providing a clearer picture and a better representation than what a client started with.

That is a takeaway that can be built on.

This book might not have the same impact if I didn't weave pieces about my own experiences, trials, and frustrations centered around my career.

Take a substance abuse counselor for example.

I would think it would be quite challenging to relate to what many of their patients are going through unless they hit rock-bottom themselves.

Right?

However, this is also not meant to be a biography, so I try to filter my history to keep it career-centric.

In closing, if you are a professional on any level struggling with career direction…

If you have come this far…

Perhaps you will go a little farther.

ABOUT THE AUTHOR

Kevin Kokinda, CPRW, CEIP, is a nationally recognized integrated career strategist, owner of Resumedics Career Strategies & Solutions, and the former host of 'The Career Maverick Podcast' and 'Clarity Thru the Chaos.'

His long and winding journeys have led to writing over 1,500 resumés. He has also served as a trusted consultant for Fortune 500 executives, a public speaker at universities, high schools, and veterans' organizations, and was selected as one of LinkedIn's 'Resumé & Career Experts in 2020.

Born in Gary, Indiana, with stints in Florida, Virginia, and Illinois, he is a US Navy veteran and a graduate of Bradley University.

He currently resides in Colorado Springs, Colorado with his wife Stacey, and three fur babies.

Acknowledgments

George A. Bonanno and Meghan Mobbs
'Beyond War and PTSD.'

Daniel Goleman
'Emotional Intelligence'

David Strayer

Paul Rupert
Respectful Exits

Gary D. Friedman and Thomas McCarthy
'Employment Law, Red Flags in the Use of Artificial Intelligence.'

His Holiness, The Dalai Lama
'Ethics For The New Millennium.'

Made in the USA
Las Vegas, NV
30 January 2022